T0113991

Cambridge Elements ≡

Elements in Publishing and Book Culture
edited by
Samantha Rayner
University College London
Leah Tether
University of Bristol

PRE-WEB DIGITAL PUBLISHING AND THE LORE OF ELECTRONIC LITERATURE

Astrid Ensslin

University of Bergen

CAMBRIDGE
UNIVERSITY PRESS

CAMBRIDGE
UNIVERSITY PRESS

University Printing House, Cambridge CB2 8BS, United Kingdom

One Liberty Plaza, 20th Floor, New York, NY 10006, USA

477 Williamstown Road, Port Melbourne, VIC 3207, Australia

314–321, 3rd Floor, Plot 3, Splendor Forum, Jasola District Centre,
New Delhi – 110025, India

103 Penang Road, #05–06/07, Visioncrest Commercial, Singapore 238467

Cambridge University Press is part of the University of Cambridge.

It furthers the University's mission by disseminating knowledge in the pursuit of
education, learning, and research at the highest international levels of excellence.

www.cambridge.org
Information on this title: www.cambridge.org/9781108828888
DOI: 10.1017/9781108903165

© Astrid Ensslin 2022

This publication is in copyright. Subject to statutory exception
and to the provisions of relevant collective licensing agreements,
no reproduction of any part may take place without the written
permission of Cambridge University Press.

First published 2022

A catalogue record for this publication is available from the British Library.

ISBN 978-1-108-82888-8 Paperback
ISSN 2514-8524 (online)
ISSN 2514-8516 (print)

Cambridge University Press has no responsibility for the persistence or accuracy of
URLs for external or third-party internet websites referred to in this publication
and does not guarantee that any content on such websites is, or will remain,
accurate or appropriate.

Pre-web Digital Publishing and the Lore of Electronic Literature

Elements in Publishing and Book Culture

DOI: 10.1017/9781108903165

First published online: March 2022

Astrid Ensslin

University of Bergen

Author for correspondence: Astrid Ensslin, astrid.ensslin@uib.no

ABSTRACT: This Element examines a watershed moment in the recent history of digital publishing through a case study of a pre-web, serious hypertext periodical, the *Eastgate Quarterly Review of Hypertext* (*EQRH*) (1994–1995). Early hypertext writing relied on stand-alone, mainframe computers and specialized authoring software. With the Web launching as a mass distribution platform, the *EQRH* faced a fast-evolving technological landscape paired with an emergent gift and open-access economy. Its nonlinear writing experiments afford key insights into historical, medium-specific authoring practices. Access constraints have left the *EQRH* under-researched and threatened by obsolescence. To address this challenge, this study offers platform-specific analyses of all of the *EQRH*'s cross-media materials, including works that have hitherto escaped scholarly attention. It deploys a form of conceptually oral ethno-historiography: the lore of electronic literature. The Element deepens our understanding of the North American publishing industry's history and contributes to the overdue preservation of early digital writing.

This Element also has a video abstract: www.cambridge.org/ensslin

KEYWORDS: Eastgate, electronic literature, hypertext, lore, pre-web digital publishing

© Astrid Ensslin 2022

ISBNs: 9781108828888 (PB), 9781108903165 (OC)

ISSNs: 2514-8524 (online), 2514-8516 (print)

Contents

1 Introduction

The late August sun streams warmly through the Venetian blinds above my desk in the Electronic Literature Lab (ELL) at Washington State University Vancouver (WSUV). A decades-old yet fully functional Macintosh Performa 5215 CD hums in front of me. In my nervously quivering hands, I hold the cool, smooth vinyl of a folio containing one of the first works of hypertext literature ever published: issue 1:1 of the *Eastgate Quarterly Review of Hypertext* (*EQRH*), a stand-alone, digital literary periodical showcasing hypertext literature produced and distributed by Eastgate Systems, Inc., between 1994 and 1995. The folio covers open with a reluctant pop, as if imploring me to respect their age and leave them untouched. I carefully wriggle out one of the 3.5-inch floppy disks squeezed into the front flap. It has "for Macintosh" printed on its sticky label. As the disk clicks into its drive, I find myself rejoicing at the all-too-familiar sound that takes me back decades – a shuttling, crackling noise that tells me in a long-forgotten, machinic code that the computer is reading the disk. I viscerally recall the sheer delight this noise used to evoke in me decades ago, and I can feel it now as poignantly as I used to – a multisensory, haptic rhythm that seems to be shaking the entire body of the computer, and with it, my hands on the worn beige plastic mouse and keyboard. On the downward flickering, black-and-white monitor display a window tells me the software is loading . . .

This Element is a work of literary digital media archeology aimed at preserving historical literary practices and material works threatened by obsolescence. It examines a watershed moment in the recent history of digital publishing: the *Eastgate Quarterly Review of Hypertext* (*EQRH*) – a stand-alone digital periodical featuring experimental forms of early, pre-web electronic literature (e-literature). The *EQRH* celebrated its twenty-fifth anniversary while I was writing this manuscript. "Serious hypertext" publisher Eastgate Systems, based in Watertown, Massachusetts, under the aegis of Mark Bernstein, curated and produced it. Its underlying agenda – to innovate short-form literary and nonliterary publishing through evolving digital technologies – was revolutionary and risky because it had no comparable commercial precedent for its business model – at least not in North

America.[1] Hypertext writing (poetry, short fiction, and scholarly nonfiction) was afforded exclusively by stand-alone, mainframe computers, early Macintoshes in particular, which came with HyperCard – a key tool for early hypertext writers. Yet, despite its innovative potential at a time when home computers became a widely accessible commodity, "serious hypertext" has been struggling to leave its niche existence.

For its production, pre-web hypertext required specialized, nonlinear, and often costly authoring software such as Hypergate, Storyspace, and HyperCard. Unlike video games and commercial print writing, it was never conceptualized as a mainstream form of entertainment and/or scholarship, which complicated the financial situation of Eastgate Systems. With the World Wide Web launching as a new mass distribution and publishing platform in the mid-1990s, it quickly became obvious that the *EQRH*'s stand-alone medial approach was subject to evanescence, despite its potential and zealous pursuit to innovate literary periodical publishing. Nonetheless, the series remains a gold mine of historical, platform-specific, nonlinear writing because it affords insights into medium-specific, creative authoring practices that reflect their scholarly paradigm in pioneering ways that heralded the transformation of literature into literary media (Hayles 2008; Thomas, Round, and Ensslin forthcoming).

Widely unavailable, the *EQRH* is notoriously under-researched and threatened by obsolescence. To make a much-needed contribution to the preservation of early, pre-web e-literature, I spent several weeks in the pre-pandemic summer of 2019 at the Electronic Literature Archive at WSUV – one of the few archives in the world that holds copies of all eight *EQRH* issues and the historical hardware devices needed to read them in the original. During my archival research, I performed so-called traversals (Moulthrop and Grigar 2017), a form of medium-specific, serendipitous yet nonetheless deep and iterative reading, of the historical material (see Section 1.2). This experience was a visceral one, allowing me to read in a fully embodied way, taking into account the multisensory,

---

[1] In France, however, the Lecture Art Innovation Recherche Ecriture (LAIRE) collective led by Philippe Bootz and Tibor Papp had already launched a transmedia and digital poetry review, *alire*, in 1989.

platform-specific interplay that is so critical to medium-specific and media-conscious analysis (Hayles 2004; Ryan and Thon 2014; Ensslin and Bell 2021).

Viewed through publishing history and hypertext theory lenses, this study offers an account of the *EQRH* as a key threshold phenomenon in recent literary publishing. Historically, the *EQRH* follows in the tradition of the modernist "little magazine" (Drouin and Huculak 2016), an experimental, niche concept that produced many short-lived periodical publications from the early twentieth century onward. While there is a host of information on how the advent of the Web in the early to mid-1990s led to a prolonged crisis of the publishing industry more broadly, there is a dearth of dedicated studies documenting how these transformations, coupled with the rapid growth of the dot.com bubble and the ascent of fourth-generation gaming platforms, affected the operations of digital literary subcultures manifesting themselves in coterie-based publishing experiments like the *EQRH*. Surely the *EQRH* was not the only experiment in literary periodical publishing at the time. Digital media zines like Adam Engst's *TidBITS* were published on floppy disk, and between 1985 and 1997, the Voyager Company pioneered film, fiction, and nonfiction on LazerDisk and CD-ROM. However, none of these competitor enterprises had as lasting and field-defining an effect as the Eastgate hypertexts did. Access issues notwithstanding, every student of e-literature and digital-born fiction will sooner or later come across the canonical work published by Eastgate, facilitated by online preservation initiatives like *Rebooting Electronic Literature* (Grigar et al. 2018; Grigar et al. 2019; Grigar et al. 2020) and web translations like Richard Holeton's *Figurski at Findhorn on Acid* (figurskiatfindhornonacid.com; Grigar et al. 2021). Although Eastgate's book-inspired stand-alone publishing model was soon replaced with web-based publications like *Tekka* and *Hypertext Reading Room*, as well as numerous other online literary magazines specializing in either paper-under-glass or more digital-born forms of writing, the legacy of the *EQRH* as an emblem of Eastgate's pivotal role in the emergent e-literature community cannot be overstated.

In Section 3, I offer analyses of all fiction, poetry, nonfiction materials, and paratextual commentaries published in the *EQRH*. They include works that have never or at best minimally been researched or written about before. This lack of attention, which paradoxically runs counter to the *EQRH*'s importance for literary media history, is a direct effect of inaccessibility. The works are only available on physical, out-of-stock disks that can only be accessed in their original forms via obsolete hardware. Characteristic of Eastgate's approach to serious hypertext publishing, the works were distributed in vinyl and cardboard folios containing print materials and electronic data carriers such as 3.5-inch floppy disks and CD-ROMs. These unique paratextual features convey a "bookish" feeling demonstrating that these media objects were meant to be put on shelves, similar to books and print journals (Pressman 2020). That this physically print-refashioning agenda would soon be overridden by the fast-evolving online and download culture of the emergent Web was barely foreseeable at the time, no matter how predictable it may appear to today's audiences.

In this introduction, I explain the conceptual and terminological framework underlying this book – particularly the decision to configure aspects of medium-specific lore for this project. I provide an overview of the theoretical lenses underpinning my work, casting light on the importance of embedding medium-specific literary history firmly within the socio-material turn of publishing and textual theory, and looking to insights from digital modernism in framing the *EQRH* and its artistic conceptualization. I close with a more detailed examination of how lore can be understood as a critical tool for subverting entrenched political and societal structures and as a systematic method of qualitative participant research.

1.1 Conceptual Framework and Terminology

According to an early (2006) definition proposed by the Electronic Literature Organization, e-literature is an art form that "works with important literary aspects that take advantage of the capabilities and contexts provided by the standalone or networked computer" (quoted in Rettberg 2019: 4). It is born digital in the sense that it is "written for and read on a computer screen [and] pursues its verbal, discursive and/or conceptual complexity through the digital medium, and would lose something of its aesthetic and semiotic function if it were removed from that medium" (Bell et al. 2010). Electronic literature pushes the boundaries of digital media's technical and material affordances, often critiquing and subverting their corporate, neoliberal underpinnings. Common experimental forms include hypertext and hypermedia; interactive fiction; literary video games and touchscreen apps; kinetic, generative, bot, and sound poetry; locative, ambient, and virtual reality/augmented reality (VR/AR) works; and social media literature such as Instapoetry and Twitterature as well as site-specific installations (Rettberg 2019). The list continuously evolves as new platforms and technologies become available, and much e-literature either programmatically defies genre categorization or becomes genre-defining retroactively.

What exactly "literature" and "literary" refer to is of course a moot point. Many works created and studied by members of the e-literature community do not have any written element to them, contrary to the original meaning of the Latin *litterae* (letters and other types of written documents) (Ensslin 2014). Some do not feature any human language at all. María Mencía's Flash poem "Birds Singing Other Birds' Songs" (2001), for example, experiments with digital birdsong as a "new poetic form of language" that transcends human communication as a reflection of its breakdown (di Rosario 2017: 274). Other works of e-literature, such as John Cayley's "riverIsland" (2007), are codeworks and/or works of combinatory poetry that foreground the source code as a poetic object and its interplay with the user interface. Yet others, like J. R. Carpenter's "Etheric Ocean" (2014), have more in common with performance art than what one may customarily associate with the private, individualized consumption of text on a page or screen.

Equally important, the elitist, Leavisite, "High Culture" undertones often associated with the term *literature* are often dismissed by e-literature scholars and artists. After all, digital technologies' evanescence is decidedly anti-canonical. A medium-conscious, digital-born notion of canon must move away from "seminal, normative and timeless" principles of canonization (Schweikle and Schweikle 1990, 232) to a more open, fluid, and nonnormative notion combining thereness, critical potential, and replicable accessibility (Ensslin 2020a). A work's existence in space, time, and community alone reflects a key moment in socio-technological history that might otherwise go unnoticed or remain undocumented.

"Literary" as a transmedial and transcultural adjective and "the literary" as a collective noun yield a much broader and more inclusive range of possible meanings than its etymological base, "literature." As Hayles (2008) suggests, "the literary" lends itself to a host of "creative artworks that interrogate the histories, contexts, and productions of literature, including as well the verbal art of literature proper" (4–5). Simultaneously, it reflects the ways in which literary media studies have become a transdisciplinary undertaking examining not only the conceptual, political, and intellectual but also the methodological conventions of media studies, cultural studies, postcolonial studies, social and data sciences, digital humanities, and many more.

Electronic literature has, over the past decade, expanded into a fully institutionalized discipline, attracting hundreds of scholars, artists, writers, curators, and media developers from around the world to its annual conferences, and building multinational, government-funded archives and databases of e-literature (CELL, ELD, and ELMCIP), as well as open-access scholarly journals like the *electronic book review* and *The Digital Review*. As a highly collaborative, multimodal trans-discipline, e-literature encapsulates multiple notions of comparative literature, in that it is multinational, multilingual, multi- and cross-platform, pre- and post-digital, as well as multimodal and – more often than not – multiauthored. In many ways, it epitomizes world literature in the sense of continuing and continually remediating a common creative practice of neo-Oulipian "writing under constraint" (Tabbi 2010). More recently, and inspired by the Black Lives Matter movement, the Electronic Literature Organization has moved its largely formalist agenda into more politicized territory – for example, by introducing bespoke fellowships to "augment anti-racism." Hence, no matter how controversial and in some ways outdated the term *literature* might seem to many, its persistence in *electronic literature* reflects the discipline's radical cultural, semiotic, and technological inclusivity and its openness to continuous innovation, nonnormativity, and transformation. In *electronic literature*, literature thus becomes both formally malleable and politically progressive, global, and inclusive.

I have settled on the use of "pre-web" to describe the works under examination because they chronologically predated the Web not as a platform for commercialization but as an outlet for creative expression and artistic innovation. Web-based hypertexts and hypermedia did not begin to proliferate until the mid-to-late 1990s, with the emergence of graphic browsers and multimedia editors like Macromedia (later Adobe) Flash. This does not mean that works published before that paradigm shift, also known as first-generation hypertexts (Hayles 2002), did not contain any graphical or color elements. As elaborated in Section 3, a surprisingly large number of works published in the *EQRH* feature pixel graphics and even some early elements of color.

The *EQRH* emerged during the early years of what is now retrospectively known as Web 1.0. As hypertext author and scholar Stuart Moulthrop put it,

> I'd call the *Eastgate Quarterly* more para-web than pre-web.
> That is, the WWW was well established when [the] *EQ*
> started up, it was publicized on the Web as well as in print,
> and the concept of highly structured hypertext that animated
> the project, at least in part, was a response to the early
> commercial Web and its "diving boards into the darkness,"
> as Ted Nelson inimitably put it. (Interview)

Moulthrop's use of "para" does not echo the meanings of Genettian paratext as the text surrounding the canonical, main text body of a novel, for example. Rather, the prefix here refers to a sense of "next-ness or approximation: parallel" (interview), signaling the coexistence of several competing models of hypertextual connectivity in the late 1980s and early 1990s that led, amongst other things, to the rejection of Tim Berners-Lee and Robert Cailliau's paper on the World Wide Web by the program committee of the 1991 ACM/Hypertext conference.

> The Web ... was only one notorious inflection of that
> concept [of links and networks]. ... There was huge regret
> about the constraints of client-server architecture. We [in
> the Eastgate hypertext community] had our elegant and
> complex flying machines and looked down our noses at

> what [we] considered clumsier mechanics. (Moulthrop,
> interview)

The third potentially puzzling element in the title of this book grew out of a conversation with hypertext scholar, archivist, and curator Dene Grigar during my archival research for this study in August 2019. In our preparations for a video interview series with emeritus scholar and hypertext philosopher David Kolb (Grigar 2019), we came to lament that a host of unpublished information circulating amongst writers, scholars, and publishers of early hypertext literature and embedded in their memories and joint nostalgic musings has never been documented in any systematic way. Capturing this "lore" requires in-depth preparation including ethical considerations as well as systematic elicitation, interviewing, recording, and participant review. All of these elements were part of this research.

Nowadays, much of the conceptually oral knowledge we associate with lore will customarily be handed down by (written or spoken) word of mouth on social media. Yet this was not the case in the early to mid-1990s, when copies of floppy disks were passed around by hand or snail mail carrier, and informal information was only beginning to be communicated via email. Hardly anybody took the pains to record spoken scholarly conversations during what are now known to be groundbreaking and field-defining conferences, such as the first Hypertext conferences starting in 1987. These events featured no lesser than Tim Berners Lee, Ted Nelson, Andries van Dam, Jeff Conklin, Peter Brown, and Douglas Engelbart, and congregated a range of literary movers and shakers around proto social media platforms (MUDs and MOOs) like *The Well* and Robert Coover's *Hypertext Hotel*.

To Eastgate founder and "serious hypertext" pioneer Mark Bernstein, the Hypertext conferences likely meant "some kind of currency" (Douglas, interview) with the emergent hypertext writing community. These events proved to be a key incubation platform for soliciting new ideas and publications as they brought together existing and new talent. In her account of how she became involved with hypertext writing, *EQRH* author and Eastgate editor Kathryn Cramer reports on its evolving digital-literary subculture thus:

I went to Hypertext '93 . . . in Seattle. . . . And it was . . . transcendent fun. [Many] Eastgate writers [were there] . . . like [Deena] Larsen, . . . Stuart Moulthrop [and] Mary Kim [Arnold]. . . . Kevin Hughes, who was actually one of the founders of the World Wide Web, . . . was part of our little [group, and so was] Brian Thomas, who did *If Monks had Macs*. . . . And we . . . . wrote this thing called the "Black Mark," . . . which we published as a kind of *samizdat* . . . of what was going on in the conference. [W]e wrote manifestos and said snarky things about what some of the presenters had said. And I was the editor of that and . . . it was . . . a very exciting time. And I remember I had not seen the World Wide Web before. Although my father had because he had the second website in the State of Washington. He's a nuclear physicist and had been at CERN; . . . so we went over to the nuclear physics lab at the University of Washington, . . . so that Kevin Hughes could show us the World Wide Web. [W]e had to actually go somewhere and do that. . . . And . . . there were papyrus scrolls or something that you could see and click on. It was like, wow. (Interview)

Cramer's memory reflects a mixture of admiration and awe for the nascent technology, and it embeds the experience in the avant-garde, subversive spirit of the emergent hypertext community at the time. Importantly, in early 1993 it was not yet clear which networked technology would eventually become mainstream. Equally critical is that the e-literature community's experimental-subversive outlook persisted then and now by exploiting and materially critiquing commercial platforms, as well as by offering its own counter-technologies.

This elucidates the pertinent, ongoing dilemma as well as an ethical, logistical, and technological challenge facing digital literary culture: the clash between the constant need and drive for innovation as a simultaneously teleological and subversive process, and the concomitant yet controversial demand for preservation. As Moulthrop and Grigar (2017) remind us, this dilemma "involves a very literal kind of rescue: the attempt to preserve fragile artistic achievements against the eroding force of obsolescence ... that will eventually affect most works of culture in the digital age" (3). The "void" opening up through ever-accelerating "technical progress" (3) threatens to swallow up hundreds if not thousands of human–machine creations every year, and I agree with Moulthrop and Grigar that it is the responsibility and duty of digital scholars to preserve as many of those works as possible because the corporate world will not do us this favor.

The *EQRH* works follow a medium-conscious and medium-reflexive agenda, providing insights into how evolving digital platforms were received and debated at the time. Second, the *EQRH* testifies to a distinct, historic "moment of possibility" (Moulthrop and Grigar 2017: 4) that arose out of the early Web and the temporary uncertainty about which technology would ultimately persist and transform into a global mass medium. This moment was decisive for the development of the Web and how we experience it today, both as a global hypermedium and as a literary-convergent platform for creative expression, experimentation, publication, reception, interaction, participation, destruction, and preservation.

1.2 Digital Modernism and Social Materialism

This study takes as its theoretical underpinnings two important streams within literary-digital culture: digital modernism and social materialism. The former seeks to distance itself from many early attempts at explaining hypertextual multi-linearity and non-closure in terms of postmodern play with subjectivities, textual deconstruction, and the demise of the author as a godlike originator of a singular work (Barthes 1977). According to Jessica Pressman, digital modernism "build[s] bridges between modernism and digital literature, print textuality and computational technologies, literary criticism and media studies" (2014: 22). Especially in early forms of e-literature, the remediation of print (Bolter and Grusin 1997) was eminently visible–despite multiple scholarly attempts to herald "the end of books" as we know them (Coover 1992), the demise of print (Bolter 1991), and the erosion of the book's hegemony in a new, hypertextual paradigm

(Landow 2006: 28). The Storyspace software, in which many Eastgate works were produced and read, even contained a "print" button, catering to a culture that struggled to imagine reading any kind of text – fictional or nonfictional – exclusively from a screen.

As Pressman (2014) elucidates, a sizable body of e-literature follows in the digital footsteps of literary modernism as represented by Ezra Pound and James Joyce. The works that most aptly lend themselves to digital modernist analysis "are text based, aesthetically difficult, and ambivalent in their relationship to mass media and popular culture. Such works offer immanent critiques of contemporary society that privileges images, naviga-tion, and interactivity over complex narrative and close readings" (Wollaeger and Dettmar 2014: ix). Their intent is to exploit and critique popular assumptions about media and their affordances, and whilst Pressman astutely places her close readings in second-generation, web-based hypermedia, her concept of digital modernism is as pertinent to first-generation, stand-alone, "serious" hypertext (see Hayles 2002; Ensslin 2007). After all, first-generation experiments were critical of the waning influence and validity of postmodernist theory as well as of book culture at the perceived brink of collapse. They refashioned "older literary practices" (Pressman 2014: 4) as well as appropriating newly evolving, digital media to explore how ideas that eluded straightforward theorization might lend themselves to the fluidity and multivalence of creative hypertextual expres-sion. In doing so, they experimented with complex designs afforded by hypertextual multilinearity, interactivity, and non-closure (see Chapter 3).

Social materialism in turn evokes Marshall McLuhan's emphasis on the medium and its material affordances and constraints. Arguing against assumptions of disembodiment of data and communication, Paul Duguid (2006) postulates an "alternative way to think of information [that] empha-sizes the role of material artifacts in both making and warranting informa-tion" (500). After all, information and the technologies used to create, encode, disseminate, and engage with it are "mutually constitutive and ultimately indissoluble" (Duguid 2006: 500). Thus, our socio-technological relations are, as Kittler (1992) would have it, part of a densely knit network of animate and inanimate participants, of humanoid and machinic intelli-gences, mechanisms, and processes that shape, embody, and transform each other entropically. Meaning, medium, and form are thus inextricably and dynamically interconnected (Chartier 1994).

If this leaves the book as a "machine to think with" (Richards 1924: vii), the perceived role of hypertext then was to embody intertextual relationships and the intrinsically networked nature of information and its social and technological agents. Hence the material turn also embedded a turn to social circuitry in textual studies (McGann 1991). With the advent of groundbreaking new, networked technologies in the second half of the twentieth century, these innovations disrupted long-standing conventional forms of communication as well as monolinear and hierarchical social processes and relationships. Therefore I must also examine how this time of great technological change transformed social interactions in publishing culture, and unwritten lore aptly fills some of the social-material gaps left by gatekept, canonical scholarship.

1.3 Methodology

My three-pronged methodological approach incorporates medium-specific textual analysis (Hayles 2004), archival research, and lore as a historical, ethnographic practice. To analyze *EQRH* works and their physical characteristics, I performed medium and platform-conscious hypertext analyses based on my traversals at ELL. A traversal is a reflective reading of a hypertext "in which the possibilities of that text are explored in a way that indicates its key features, capabilities, and themes" (Moulthrop and Grigar 2017: 7). To allow for authentic, embodied reading experiences, traversals "must take place on equipment configured as closely as possible to the system used to create the work or on which the work might have been expected to reach its initial audience" (ibid.: 7). As indicated in the opening paragraph to this book, this embodied reading is multisensory and not only takes into account visual and haptic aspects of user interface interaction but also includes the sensory effects of vintage hardware soundscapes like "the whirring and clicking of the floppy drive, a kind of mechanical theme song" (ibid.: 7). Traversals of historical e-literature works thus call out for a platform-specific phenomenological and hermeneutic approach integrating the analysis of both interface design and the historical physical hardware infrastructure that readers and authors at the time would have been embedded in. I read the original *EQRH* works on an archival Macintosh Performa 5215 CD, a model that came with a 75 MHz PowerPC 603 processor, 8 MB of RAM, a 1.0 GB hard drive, and a 4X CD-ROM Drive (madeApple.com 2020) and was produced and distributed between July 1995 and July 1996. It generically ran System Software 7.5.1 and maxed at Mac OS 9.1.

To replicate my reading paths and write about the *texte-à-voir* (on-screen text spaces or lexias; Bootz 2005) in more detail, I performed further back-up readings on my own Alienware PC, enabled by VirtualBox JavaScript emulation. My analyses are further enriched by archival research using the catalogues and publications of the ELL and the Pathfinders Project (Grigar and Moulthrop 2017), combined with the Electronic Literature Directory, the ELMCIP Knowledge Base, and other e-literature databases. During this complementary archival process, I helped develop these crowdsourced, moderated, and peer-to-peer reviewed databases by creating new and updating existing entries on the site-specific primary works, thus preserving and documenting them for broader public audiences.

I further set out to fill the gaps left by existing research on early, pre-web hypertext by using the "lore of electronic literature" (Grigar 2019). Lore is based on storytelling and personalized memory, binding its agents together by a keen sense of shared interest or experiential background even while subjective accounts of one and the same event, place, interpersonal relationship, or time period will likely differ. In many ways, then, this study frames the early e-literature community as a modern, techno-aesthetic tribe that has been operating largely outside of the confines of commercialized pop culture, yet relied on the dictates of late capitalism for its existence and cohesion.

By adopting lore as a research object and method, I consciously enter controversial scholarly territory. Yet literary communication and meta-communication, no matter the medium, are "part of a social process, … a kind of intervention in a continuous discourse, debate, and conflict about power and social relations" (Zipes 2006: 2). Likewise the lore of e-literature feeds into and documents this ideological agenda and critically engages with the kinds of economically, materially, and aesthetically "unresolvable contradictions" facing its community, then and now. To study the free-floating lore of e-literature, I followed a systematic qualitative-ethnographic trajectory. To elicit conceptually oral insider information from the first-generation hypertext community, I interviewed, between June 2018 and October 2020, thirteen key contributors to the *EQRH*: Mary-Kim Arnold, Mark Bernstein, Kathryn Cramer, J. Yellowlees Douglas, Edward Falco, Richard Gess, Robert Kendall, Deena Larsen, Kathy Mac, Stuart Moulthrop, Jim Rosenberg, Richard Smyth, Rob Swigart, and Michael van Mantgem. They answered the same list of questions in written form, via email, or orally via videoconferencing:

1. What, in your perception, were the main goals / motivations / rationale behind the *Eastgate Quarterly Review of Hypertext*?
2. How did the *EQRH* come into being?
3. In your recollection, what business model did the *EQRH* follow?
4. How were contributions solicited and/or how were IP and royalties handled?
5. How were copies of the *EQRH* produced and disseminated?
6. The *EQRH* was discontinued after two full years. What do you think were the main reasons for its short-lived existence, and how would you describe the (digital) publishing landscape at the time that brought about its sudden rise and demise?
7. Please share your personal experiences and memories of engaging with the *EQRH*, as author, editor, reader, etc..
8. Can you see a future of the *EQRH*? If so, what might it look like?

These questions were intended to trigger specific memories in relation to the *EQRH* as a publication enterprise, as well as memories relating to the technological and publishing landscape in the early-to-middle 1990s. Further informants, who generously provided additional background details about Eastgate and the early hypertext community via Zoom, Discord, and oral communication, included former Eastgate editor Diane (Greco) Josefowicz, e-literature preservationist Dene Grigar, hypertext author Michael Joyce, and his former student Heather Malin.

Most of the information I gathered in this way has not been previously documented or published elsewhere. It provides conceptual material for filling the gaps left by existing scholarship and includes discursive insights about how these early authors, publishers, and editors now position themselves in relation to the events and settings they experienced. I directly quote participants' responses wherever possible because they convey narrative information that exceeds the "factual." They reveal a strong sense of stance and affect – which are often edited out in scholarly discourse and yet are so important for gaining a rounded and sometimes conflicted view of personal and communal historical experience.

Overall, this study offers a multifaceted, plurivocal understanding of a historic yet fleeting moment in the late twentieth-century publishing industry. Chapter 2 examines the media-historical dilemma of the *EQRH*, highlighting Mark Bernstein's and Eastgate's critical role and documenting the ways in which his particular vision translated into practices of solicitation, author liaison, contractual matters, packaging, distribution, PR and communications. Chapter 3 zooms in on the *EQRH* itself as an experimental platform for new hypertext forms and genres and provides platform-specific analyses of its primary material, including hitherto undocumented and under-documented works. In the concluding chapter, I evaluate the lasting significance of the *EQRH* and explore some ideas of where small e-literary publishing is headed now and in the years to come.

2 Between Paradigms

2.1 Publishing at the Turn of the Millennium

Bernstein's "idea of the [*EQRH*] grew from two sources: [Eastgate's]
view of the immediate future of literary hypertext in the context of the
early 1990s, and the challenges confronting publishing in that era" (interview). The late 1980s and early 1990s were a "crucial moment in the
cultural history of computing" (Moulthrop and Grigar 2017: 8) that saw
a shift from first-generation personal computers to a second wave that
introduced key innovations such as the computer mouse as the first
clickable pointing device, graphical user interfaces, and bitmapped
screens. These advances paved the way for the "popularization of the
Internet and the World Wide Web, bringing an emphasis on color
graphics, complex visual design, and a notably constrained version of
hypertext" (ibid. 2017: 8). Web-based hypertext was essentially mono-
directional and designed to give users direct access to the information
they expected behind a hyperlink. For writers and artists, however,
networked textuality provided an ideal breeding ground and experimental sandbox for aesthetic play with intertextuality, connectivity, materiality, cyclicality, agency, failure, unreliability, fragmentation, spatial
composition, and (non-)closure.

For literary scholars and writers, the early 1990s were further shaped
by the intellectual imprint of postmodernism and poststructuralism.
Concepts like rhizomatic thought (Deleuze and Guattari 1987), deconstruction and decentering, the death of the author, the lexia as textual
component (Barthes 1970), intertextuality, and heteroglossia dominated
scholarly discourse, and so for many in this community, this period was
"a time of great anticipation and intellectual ferment around the possibilities of hypertext as a direct manifestation of the literary theory popular
at the time" (Richard Smyth, interview). In other words, George
Landow's (1997) much-debated convergence thesis, which frames hypertext as embodiment or instantiation of poststructuralist theory, ought to
be seen not as a scholarly idiosyncrasy, but as a reflection of a belief
shared by many at the time.

The pending arrival of the Web instilled a great sense of fear and uncertainty in print-centered literary commerce:

> The literary world of the 90s was deeply anxious. Customs and practices that had long endured were vanishing; Hollywood and New York, once rival cultural poles, were now teamed together in multimedia conglomerates. Publishers consolidated; storied imprints disappeared. Computers offered booksellers all sorts of promise, not least of which was the hope – for the first time in memory – of actually understanding what was selling while there was still time to sell more. But computers had screens, and screens – movie screens, and then television – were thought to be stealing the remnants of the literary audience. (Bernstein, interview)

These economical anxieties surrounding the looming "End of Books" were nurtured and extrapolated in Robert Coover's 1992 essay in the *New York Times*. The article elucidates the "feverish moribundity" of print and the "demise" of the traditional novel. It pitches hypertext as a liberational, "radically divergent" technology, "interactive and polyvocal, favoring a plurality of discourses over definitive utterance and freeing the reader from domination by the author." Little did his readers know, of course, how great and lasting the popular resistance to this liberational moment would ultimately be. Yet for the publishing industry, Coover's narrative epitomized the need to rethink its century-old business models. A paradigm shift was on the horizon, and it was not going to be confined to sales, distribution, and marketing.

It was in this changing paradigm that Mark Bernstein, variably referred to as "chemist" (he has a PhD in chemistry from Harvard), "chief scientist," and "small shopkeeper," founded Eastgate Systems Inc. in Watertown, Massachusetts, in 1982. Eastgate was conceptualized as a software and publishing company, and its main products have been the hypertext authoring tool, Storyspace, the personal content management system Tinderbox, and, starting in 1987, a large repository of so-called serious hypertext

spanning fiction, poetry, and nonfiction. Eastgate's canonical and lesser
known yet equally important works are listed in its online catalog, and they
have been archived at institutions like WSUV and the Maryland Institute
for Technology in the Humanities, the Library of Congress, and the
Ransom Center.

Eastgate's vision was to be a site of experimentation and innovation in
the fast-changing publishing world. It positioned itself as a provider of
hypertext – albeit more in a technological than a literary sense. Yet to its
reading and writing audiences, Eastgate's arguably greatest achievement
was to:

> help disseminate and legitimize hypertext *literature*. The
> Web wasn't yet a significant vehicle for literature, so
> Eastgate was really the only game in town if you wanted
> readers for your electronic writing. Robert Coover's
> New York Times article ... turned Eastgate into a sort of
> avant-garde icon. Coover pushed hypertext as the ultimate
> realization of the poststructuralist desire to turn the reader
> into the author, so this made hypertext fiction a hot com-
> modity for a time. And Eastgate became synonymous with
> hypertext fiction. So Mark Bernstein ... was quite successful
> in raising the profile of and generating readership for these
> early works. He was able to give works of electronic litera-
> ture the same status as printed books, though they never had
> a very broad readership. (Kendall, interview; emphasis
> mine)

I first encountered hypertext as an inherently Eastgate-driven phenomenon
during my early months in graduate school at the University of Tübingen,
Germany, in the late 1990s. Surely Bernstein's endeavors had been success-
ful enough to reach academic audiences far beyond North America and to
inspire entire course designs and scholarly conferences on European territory and elsewhere.

Yet Eastgate's business model also addressed an imminent challenge
facing booksellers at the time:

the problem of size. A significant part of any bookstore's sales are current best-sellers that are displayed in store windows and on the front table. The demand for space in those windows shapes many aspects of literary life . . . But in the late 20th century, it created strong pressures toward very small or very large bookstores, and these pressures quickly overwhelmed everything else. (Bernstein, interview)

Eastgate's material affiliations with the bookselling trade are reflected in the makeup of its products and the fact that their folios were adorned with in-house cover designs shipped for on-shelf display and pitched to booksellers directly, often via physical promotion visits.

Another significant challenge facing Eastgate was the question of scope, which was critical to reader appreciation and formal-material concerns:

A pressing question for us in the early 1990s was, what is the natural size of a hypertext? We had no obvious precedent, or perhaps we had too many. The size of the novel was one landmark, but this size had resulted from a complex array of commercial forces. . . . A vital marketplace in freestanding short literature had flourished in early modern Europe. . . . Much of the work sold by rack jobbers was short, and this was subject to constant experimentation. (Bernstein, interview)

In the late twentieth century, the market for short literary forms was lean at best, and mostly fed into literary education in schools. Hence, unsurprisingly, Bernstein's original assumption was that hypertext narratives should or would be of novelistic length or even longer. However, he confesses that "that assumption was arbitrary, and it was shaken by two short works that arrived at about the same time: Mary-Kim Arnold's 'Lust' and Kathryn Cramer's 'In Small & Large Pieces.' 'Lust' is at once tiny and intricate; it would have been impossible to ignore even without Robert Coover's glowing recommendation, itself impossible to ignore" (Bernstein, interview). This observation suggests that the idea for launching a publication dedicated to shorter, experimental forms of hypertext emerged partly inductively, from the need to find a platform of Arnold's and Cramer's works that would give them due visibility. It also explains why issue 1:2 of the *EQRH*, which integrated both works, entered production before issue 1:1, containing Jim Rosenberg's *Intergrams*.

The *EQRH* was by no means the only idea on the table at the time. As Moulthrop reminds us, "the idea of a hypertextual journal or review was something lots of people were kicking around in the 1980s. I remember pitching a 'Forking Paths Review' to Richard Lanham, who correctly pointed out that I should try never naming anything" (interview). Moulthrop's concept was one of many that did not see the light of day, and yet, evidently, a platform that would allow short-form experimentation, particularly by aspiring, new talent, to reach broader audiences seemed in order at the time. Bernstein elaborates the distinct formal implications of this experimental drive thus:

> [S]ome craft concerns in early hypertext fiction seemed best addressed in short form. How did geometry and narrative fuse in what Bolter called architectonic writing? What could we say in the space between writing spaces, in the imaginative space the link creates in the chasm between one lexia and another, or in the montage created by the juxtaposition of two distinct writing spaces? How can we talk about and improve pacing and rhythm in a hypertext that offers myriad different paths? How does first-person voice or free indirect discourse interact with the (constrained, contingent) agency of the reader armed with a mouse? . . . These topics seemed apt for exploration in compact fiction, if only compact fiction could reach an audience. . . . Then there was the question of poetry. It was clear from the outset that poets would do interesting things with computers, and the things they were doing looked hypertextual. I expected the poets would lead and everyone would follow, that poetry would again be where it all began. We wanted Eastgate to support that conversation. (Interview)

As I elaborate in Chapter 3, the critical role of poetry in driving hyper-textual experimentation was to challenge formalist standards of narrativity. The fascination with this new technology inspired emergent writers like Kathryn Cramer to leave Columbia University and work for Eastgate in the Boston area. Eastgate's appeal was countercultural from the outset. To this day, it publicly frames itself as "a small company" and it never employed "more than a handful of employees" (Cramer, interview). With "offices ... located in a historic eighteenth-century farmhouse that was once a funeral home (lots of interesting passageways; more than a few bumps in the night) ... [and that had] a circle of mushrooms growing on the floor" (interview) at times, it exerted a curious appeal to the young Cramer.

Eastgate's extraordinary courage and entrepreneurism at a time when "few other publishers in the United States were willing or able to produce literature that required viewers to load files onto computers" (Funkhouser 2007: 153) marked the beginnings of what is now an established, flourishing field within digital arts. In fact, it is impossible to imagine any of its community's past and present achievements without acknowledging the critical role played by Eastgate and Mark Bernstein at the time.

2.2 Digi-modernist Little Magazine

In many ways, the *EQRH* followed in the footsteps of the modernist "little magazine" (also called "small" magazine), a "high-minded [and often short-lived] literary undertaking that assumed sometimes enormous financial risk for an ideal of promoting and contributing to one's own literary culture" (Waterman 2009). As an outlet for new talent and new works of renowned authors alike, little magazines were and continue to be periodical publications aimed primarily at publishing short-form "serious literature" (Drouin and Huculak 2016), including poetry, serialized novels, short stories, dramatic scenes, reviews, essays, scientific literature, and reader correspondence. They were and still are noncommercial and experimental in ideology and audience orientation, "in opposition to large commercial magazines whose content is strongly influenced by markets" (Drouin and Huculak 2016).

By the late 1900s, hundreds of literary periodicals had been launched, which was partly due to the expansion of academic creative writing programs in the United States and the UK in the final quarter of the century. Yet with the dawn of the Web on the horizon, the question occurred how this somewhat "frenzied literary output" (Waterman 2009) might find a venue "for its tenuous existence" (ibid.) in digital media. With Eastgate acting as an "avant-garde icon" (Kendall, interview) of the early post-print era, coupled with its trademark motto to publish "serious hypertext," the *EQRH* may thus be considered an "electronic answer to ... the little magazines where most serious American poetry and short fiction ... appeared [from the early twentieth century onward], [such as] *Prairie Schooner*, say, or *Triquarterly*" (Richard Gess, interview). Interestingly, both *Prairie Schooner* and *Triquarterly* have adapted to the changing media landscape by making content downloadable and providing alternatives to print such as podcasts, blog posts, and videos. The para-web approach followed by Eastgate Systems, however, remained situated in a Web 1.0 framework of audience engagement, restraining many-to-many interaction and eschewing participatory culture as a deliberate intellectual and ideological choice.

Thus, as digital-modernist little magazine par excellence, the *EQRH* embodied the existential evanescence of the modernist little magazine a lot more authentically than many of its contemporaries did, and it continued its presence well into the Web 2.0 paradigm and to the present day. With its insistence on alternative, non-immersive hypertextual experimentalism, novelty, and estrangement, as well as its resistance to the massification of content, form, as well as authoring, reading, and trade conventions, it embraced its subcultural identity. To the present day, it has cultivated "a community of dedicated followers" (Drouin and Huculak 2016) who identify with Eastgate's coterie spirit in the sense of a "shared interest in radical aesthetics and politics" (ibid.). Yet Eastgate also alienated a lot of its followers by pursuing this agenda, especially those trying to make its works accessible to educational audiences in classrooms and library settings. After all, charging readers for mail-ordered material in regions close to commercially traded entertainment software ($49.95 was the asking price for four issues of the *EQRH*) seems curiously out of line with its otherwise digi-avant-garde setup.

2.3 Product Concept and Business Model

The main goal of the *EQRH* was "to provide a [visionary and unique] platform for those attempting to invent new forms of literary output, . . . [as] a way to demonstrate the promise of hypertext as theorized [by the likes of Landow and Bolter]. . . . There aren't many venues for such publications, even today (that I know of)" (Smyth, interview). At the time of my research, the Eastgate website handled information about the *EQRH* in a somewhat cryptic fashion, framing individual issues in terms of the hypertexts published in them rather than as a cohesive periodical publication (see Figure 1). Subscription is evidently no longer an option, but more generally, there is little information to be gleaned about the *EQRH* and its (historical) goals and contents from the Eastgate website.

By contrast, a variety of small publisher directories from the late 1990s and 2000s convey a clearer picture of Eastgate's digi-modernist agenda. For example, the *Directory of Poetry Publishers* (2006–2007, and many years preceding that volume), lists the *EQRH*, including address details, commissioning, and submission information. It explains that the publication "[e]xpects 1–2 poems 2006, [and] 1–2 poems 2007," suggesting that, even a decade after its discontinuation, there was still a common understanding that Eastgate was actively soliciting material, albeit restricted to "[h]ypertextual poetry only." The entry advises authors that submission guidelines are available from the Eastgate website, and it lists the subscription price at $49.49 and the price per copy at $19.95. The *EQRH* here frames itself as interested in unpublished poets and as accepting of simultaneous submissions, and it lists Edward Falco and Stephanie Strickland as "recently published poets." Evidently, the latter is inaccurate as the *EQRH* never did publish any work by Strickland, although Eastgate itself did (*True North*, 1997). In terms of special interests, the entry says that "[t]he editor is interested in translations," another ambition that never came to fruition in the *EQRH*. Finally, and most quirkily, the entry closes with the editor's emphatic mission statement: "Everything we publish could be construed as 'experimental.' No light verse, *nothing* sentimental – there is nothing worse than going for unearned emotional effect." If these words are indeed Bernstein's, they convey the "chief scientist's" explicit and unconditional

I have said nothing

By J. Yellowlees Douglas.

$24.95

Macintosh/Windows

Bracketed by two fatal car accidents, "I Have Said Nothing" is a meditation on the enormity that divides us from others.

read more

add to cart

Unnatural Habitats

By Kathy Mac.

$24.95

Macintosh/Windows

Canadian poet Kathy Mac explores the consequences of American idealism, from the Apollo 13 tragedy, to the U.S. invasion of Kuwait.

read more

add to cart

Completing The Circle

By Michael van Mantgem.

$24.95

Macintosh/Windows

Would you like to experience a scotomic episode? Click here.

read more

add to cart

Lust

By Mary-Kim Arnold.

$24.95

Macintosh/Windows

This bold work uses the limits of this new form to great advantage. One of the most influential hypertexts yet written: "A miniature gem". – New York Times Book Review.

read more

add to cart

Mothering

By Judith Kerman.

$24.95

Macintosh/Windows

Sensitive, whimsical and moving. The continual sound – part murmur, part jackhammer – of a mother's voice binds past, present, and possible futures.

read more

add to cart

A Life Set for Two

By Robert Kendall and Richard Smyth.

$24.95 Windows

Welcome to Café Passé. Place a retrospective order and discover how regret, desire, bitterness and memory feed on dreams. Don't forget to leave room for dessert.

read more

add to cart

In Small & Large Pieces

By Kathryn Cramer.

$24.95

Macintosh/Windows

A postmodern Through the Looking Glass. Anna's parents have that bad habit of falling apart in a crisis.

read more

add to cart

Century Cross

By Deena Larsen.

$24.95

Macintosh/Windows

What happens when a technical writer for a government agency locks herself overnight in the Federal Center to catch up on her work? Coyote pays a visit.

read more

add to cart

Genetis

By Richard Smyth.

$24.95

Macintosh/Windows

After the narrator's mental meltdown on his honeymoon, he learns that only writing has this power to salvage his sanity and his life.

read more

add to cart

Figure 1 Screenshot from the Eastgate website, featuring individual *EQRH* works, July 28, 2020

passion about his digi-modernist agenda and his equally strongly felt aversion to mainstream literary culture.

The International Directory of Little Magazines & Small Presses of 1999–2000 gives partly discrepant information about the *EQRH*, referring to a much broader scope of genres that Bernstein must have considered appropriate for this publication: "poetry, fiction, articles, art, photos, interviews, satire, criticism, parts-of-novels, long-poems, collages, non-fiction." The double requirement that Eastgate was accepting "electronic submissions only; send disks, not paper," and that "[w]orks should be in some way 'hypertextual' (loosely construed)" speaks volumes about the publisher's medium-conscious agenda that likely appealed to a select few at the time. The commercial pricing, on the other hand, was coupled with discounts and site licenses offered by Eastgate, possibly to encourage educational uses.

Michael Joyce, author of *afternoon, a story*, hypothesizes that Bernstein likely "invented the review as a way to publish what he considered minor works, doing so to promote the Eastgate list" (personal correspondence, August 1, 2018). Bernstein became aware of these minor works at Hypertext and other tech conferences where they were exhibited or demonstrated, through personal recommendations from supervisors and friends, and (self-)nominations, again typically at conferences. Bernstein thus married his motivation to promote the work of students and aspiring writers with a subscription model aimed to generate a more steady income flow. With its accelerated, serialized publishing activity, the *EQRH* lent itself to a convenient catalogue approach, including "a few ads here and there" (Falco, interview). The catalogue was shipped with mail-ordered hypertexts or individually, as fold-up fliers, as documented by Figure 2, from Richard Smyth's personal collection.

With the catalogue mailers, Bernstein intended to strengthen his "handselling staple: 'Trust me and read this; it's that good'" (interview). He followed that approach consistently by promoting Eastgate publications onsite, to booksellers, via personal pitching and marketing advice.

2.4 Material Forms and Processes

Like other Eastgate products, the *EQRH* featured hypertexts created in Storyspace or HyperCard. The former is Eastgate's proprietary software

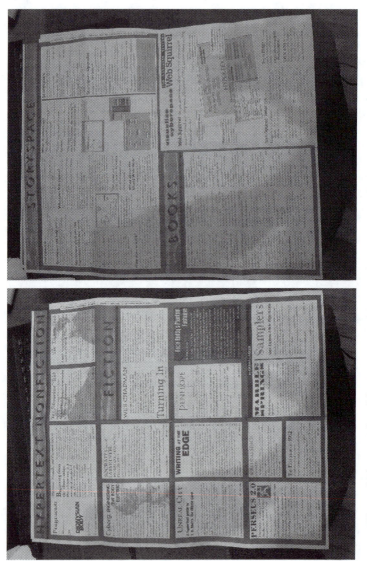

Figure 2 Photographs of the Eastgate catalogue mailer, summer 1997, courtesy of Richard Smyth

for Windows and Macintosh, launched in 1987 and available to the present day. HyperCard, on the other hand, was a default application shipped with Macintosh computers from 1987 to 2004. As noted in Chapter 3, HyperCard provided an unprecedented range of creative tools, including multimodal designs and interactivity that went well beyond hyperlinks.

The *EQRH* hypertexts were stored on 3.5-inch floppy disks and later CDs and wooden flash drives, with versions for both Macintosh and Windows saved on separate data carriers. As Cramer reports from her time as Eastgate's editor, customer service manager, and cover art and type designer,

> Barbara Bean [Eastgate's office manager] would sit there and she would duplicate discs. And there were folders they were put in . . . and Barbara would wrap these things in the shrink wrap plastic and would run the hairdryer over it and then we would have the inventory on the shelf, so . . . we did not send them out for being duplicated. They were duplicated in-house . . .. The covers were professionally printed. And I talked Mark into . . . transitioning out of those ugly plastic [vinyl] binders and into the nicer looking [paperwhites]."

From a preservational point of view, the move to cardboard paperwhites was a fortunate decision as it increased the durability and usability of the contents of each folio.

The *EQRH* issues contained between one and three original works. The pairing concept was likely intended "to increase the appeal to readers by giving them more for their money" (Kendall, interview). The cover art resulted in a series of colorful designs, depicted in Figure 3.

Eastgate's sales concept for the *EQRH* was aligned with the standard book and periodical subscription and mail-order model. However, the newly evolving "intersection of literature and software in the early 1990s" (Bernstein, interview) posed a core problem to publishers, which was the question of how to distribute the material and what business models to draw inspiration from:

Figure 3 Cover designs of all eight *EQRH* issues

[H]ow would people find and buy what you published? Some placed early bets on electronic *samizdat*, and a few zines flourished on floppy disk. Adam Engst's TidBITS is still around, and so in a sense is Gareth Branwyn's "Beyond Cyberpunk." Sams Publishing, possessing an established channel of tech retailers, tried using it for software publishing. Broderbund bet on software stores and catalogers. Infocom tried to teach software stores about the virtues of a backlist, a strategy the Activision acquisition undid. Voyager had film money, but its eyes were on bookstores. . . .

The Quarterly drew inspiration from one of America's great literary successes, Harry Scherman's Book of the Month Club. Book publishers have seldom established a brand. . . . When you visit a bookstore, you might see a sign for NEW FICTION or EUROPEAN HISTORY, but you seldom see a bookcase for RANDOM HOUSE or LITTLE, BROWN & CO. . . . [F]or decades, Book of the Month sold books because they were books of the month; the club served as bookstore clerk to people who couldn't visit bookstores. Eastgate thought that might work: we'd select good hypertexts – we worked hard at acquisitions and editing – and our recommendation might be good enough for our audience. It would be a small and specialized audience, of course, but that was not a bad thing.

Eastgate's sales strategy included the targeting of bookstores with whom the publisher hoped to forge close links for promotion and advertising, but also to provide an intellectual backdrop that would lend the brand credibility amongst learned audiences:

If nothing else, bookstores could help bestow a cultural imprimatur, an assurance that these hypertexts were literary work. That mattered to our readers, and perhaps mattered even more to our writers. . . . Eastgate was tiny and under-capitalized, and we worried that a better-funded rival could

> block our distribution. . . . Much of what we did was intended
> to make hypertexts safe for bookstores; our packages had
> spines so you could shelve them, they had covers so they'd
> look good on a table, our hypertexts were priced like books
> and they were advertised (far too sparsely) in places like the
> New York Times Book Review. (Bernstein, interview)

Eastgate authors' public bookstore readings then introduced audiences to entirely new and entertaining models of shared literary performance. As Cramer recalls, "I would have an absolute blast . . . And I would . . . have the audience [help me pick where we were going], and it was really, really fun" (interview). Yet, despite the innovative potential of short-form hypertext delivered by Eastgate, Bernstein was acutely aware of the potentially short-lived nature of booksellers' support for short fiction and poetry sales:

> For more than a generation, booksellers had struggled to sell
> short stories. They tried collections, anthologies, monthlies,
> quarterlies, cheap editions, fine printings, artist books. They
> tried celebrity events, readings, television shows, parties,
> happenings. Nothing had worked. (Interview)

Eastgate's lean economic circumstances placed further constraints on its in-house operations. Cramer recalls "the upstairs room where Mark was [and] where Barbara [Bean's] desk was . . ., and then there was my desk downstairs" (interview), where Cramer worked with assistant editor Diane Greco. Eastgate employees always answered customer support calls directly by telephone and email, and although occasionally "sales would fall short and Mark would say, 'Can you work fewer hours?'" Cramer remembers Eastgate as "a pretty happy place" with a strong sense of collegiality and a shared passion for its joint work and mission.

2.5 Copyright, Contracts, and Royalties

For the publishing industry, the late 1990s was a time of uncertainty, leading publishers and authors to question the future of print as a technology and cultural paradigm. At a time that immediately preceded the digital publishing revolution, new trading, marketing and sales models like freemium, open access, print-on-demand, as well as downloadable and upgradable content were on the horizon. So was the birth of the copyleft movement, with Creative Commons becoming the new standard for digital publishing and sharing. The inherently public nature and growing gift culture of the Web increasingly allowed if not compelled digital writers "to make their works freely available if they wanted them to be read more widely" (Ensslin and Skains 2017: 297), which was diametrically opposed to the more copyright-leaning intellectual property model followed by Eastgate.

In line with its dedication to more traditional bookselling models, Eastgate followed a rigorous editorial process. As Smyth recalls,

> An editor was assigned to my project ... who was very careful about IP ... concerns, asking me to revise the work. In fact, we [Smyth and his graphic designer Roy Parkhurst] had originally used music that was copyrighted, so we created the visuals incorporated into our piece [Genetis], asked a friend to compose original music so that we weren't in violation of copyright. I also remember being asked to add "footnotes" ... for quotations used in the piece ... to avoid copyright issues. (Interview)

Surely, then, for publications that were subject to the economic dictates of late print culture, a juridically conservative approach seemed appropriate, no matter how counterintuitive it felt to its experimental writers.

Closely linked to questions of copyright was that of royalties, and this is where participants in my survey seemed to disagree significantly. In line with a "standard print publisher's business model" (Kendall), most of them recall signing a contract "of some kind" (Smyth). However, this level of legal formality was not consistently maintained. Bernstein did or did not countersign author contracts. If he did, it was as "President" of Eastgate (a matter of state law) rather than "Chief Scientist," which suggests fluidity in editorial identity, depending on legal requirements. Furthermore, contracts did not always state a due date, conveying a somewhat relaxed attitude toward committing authors to the delivery of their material.

This hands-off approach was also visible in the royalties section. Some authors confirmed negotiating and/or receiving royalty cheques worth 10 percent of the sales and/or a $100 advance. But receipt of the money was inconsistent, and some took issue or even considered legal action over this. Others, like Kathy Mac, did not query the lack of remuneration: "You have to remember: I'm a poet. I never expect to get royalties, let alone an advance" (interview). Indeed, some fledgling authors felt "so flattered to be in print [they] didn't want any money" (Douglas, interview). Again others, like Cramer, did not sign away their copyright at the time. However, with the benefit of hindsight Cramer concedes that, "if I redid it now, I would launch it via Eastgate, rather than trying to take it somewhere else, because it is the authentic thing that was part of that era" (interview).

In sum, then, the plight of the *EQRH* reflects many Eastgate writers' understanding that their engagement with hypertext never did or would become a financially viable project. Whilst for most it was "more a labour of love than anything, . . . for [Bernstein] it was some residual way [to make] a living" (Douglas) out of the lean revenues generated by the sales of Storyspace and later Tinderbox. Conversely, for writers of the Eastgate School, writing for the *EQRH* involved "an enormous amount of generosity . . . in terms of sharing interesting work or resources" (ibid.), which can be considered a harbinger of the dawning e-literary gift economy.

2.6 Building a Community

The mutual generosity between Eastgate writers was and still is an important part and trademark of the e-literature community. Nevertheless, developing this community spirit, with multidirectional links and effective information and technological exchange, was no small feat when the fastest and most accessible way of communicating was via landline telephone, especially if email addresses were unknown. Many hypertext writers never met each other in person. As Douglas remembers, on one occasion she was frantically trying to phone Storyspace co-creators Jay D. Bolter and Michael Joyce while she was working with a fragile 1.0 beta version of the software, an experience further aggravated by a not-too-minor incident at her house:

> And when it started crashing, I couldn't get a hold of Jay. And
> at one point, when my house was burning down, I was calling,
> literally the fire department was coming. ... And Jay said,
> "you have to call me back in thirty minutes" (ignoring the fact
> that my house was on fire). . . . So I fell back on finding all the
> Michael Joyces I could in a phone book . . . He was in Jackson,
> Michigan, and ... I went to the University of Michigan. ...
> And I think on my fourth Michael Joyce, I got the right one.
> And so we all got connected up in a weird way. And we all
> went to Eastgate because we all knew each other and we knew
> Mark very loosely, but Eastgate is also the only outlet where
> we could possibly have published any of this stuff. (Interview)

Bernstein was acutely aware of Eastgate's monopoly on serious hypertext
publishing at the time. In his role as gatekeeper and incentivizer, he
nurtured connections and interactions between potential contributors. As
Mary-Kim Arnold recalls,

> I remember Mark organizing a couple events that I read and
> spoke at. It's possible Eastgate might have supported my
> travel to the 1993 Hypertext Conference in Seattle where
> I met other hypertext authors. The world of publishing and
> academic conferences was all very new to me – I was just
> finishing up my undergraduate degree. (Interview)

This feeling was shared by more established writers and academics like
Edward Falco, who drew inspiration from interchanges with like-minded
experimental writers with a keen interest in the material exploitation of
writing technologies and the limits of verbal composition:

> I met Mark Bernstein, Stuart Moulthrop, Michael Joyce,
> Stephanie Strickland, and many other gifted writers with
> an interest in "experimental" writing, especially writing
> created for reading on computers. It was an exciting time
> for imagining ways of designing and creating nonlinear

> writing, writing that was able to move in multiple directions
> navigated by the reader. (Interview)

Bernstein's contribution to network formation and the disruption of imagined and real hierarchies between established e-literature writers and scholars and new talent was critical, particularly in the absence of social media and other Web 2.0 participatory infrastructure. The technologies produced and traded by Eastgate themselves provided the grounds for an evolving community of practice as they centered around Storyspace as a key hypertext authoring tool. "Storyspace … had a centripetal force amongst a lot of us, because it was a great platform and it does things that Ted Nelson [was] trying to get Xanadu to get to do … on a 64 K Mac that only had one external disk drive" (Douglas, interview). The perceived connective potential of Storyspace at the time can thus be considered an ideologically opposed forerunner to the controversial business models of today's social media conglomerates.

The Eastgate community members called this proto-social media distribution network "sneakernet":

> Everywhere you went, you'd just hand somebody a floppy
> disk. … I met up with somebody who was at Heriot-Watt at
> the time to write a chapter for an edited collection. And
> I handed him a copy of Storyspace (the most recent ver-
> sion), [and we] realized the extent to which some of this stuff
> could spread quite quickly, without … any kind of formal
> network for distribution. (Douglas, interview)

Thus, with the *EQRH* and its networking and solicitation practices, Eastgate and its authors laid the foundation to an important social aspect that characterizes the e-literature community to the present day.

2.7 Between a Rock and a Hard Place

The sheer speed at which the *EQRH* rose and fell between its editorial beginnings in 1993 and its final issue in 1995 may seem surprising at first, even for a little magazine. Yet its heightened activity can be linked to

Eastgate's editorial staff doubling in summer 1994, when Diane Greco Josefowicz was hired to assist Kathryn Cramer. "During that summer we acquired many if not most of the titles subsequently published in the *EQRH*" (Greco, personal correspondence, February 15, 2021). Eastgate published most of *EQRH*'s issues between fall 1994 and fall 1997, and its activity dropped significantly when Greco took up a fellowship at the Dibner Institute for the History of Science to finish her PhD in late 1997.

The periodical was listed in small publishers' directories until well after the final issue. Similarly, in *Othermindedness: The Emergence of Network Culture* (2000), Michael Joyce refers to his dissertation student Heather Malin's hypertext "contour and consciousness" (1999) as forthcoming in the *EQRH*. Arguably, had there been a Volume 3, it might have been published there although, even at the time of writing Joyce's book, a continuation after a three- or four-year break must already have seemed unlikely.

The *EQRH*'s sudden demise wasn't surprising for other reasons, given the high-risk nature of the enterprise that set any editors' stakes high and required an enormous amount of visionary spirit, leadership, and personal sacrifice: "Sustaining any serial publication takes heroic work; journals fail even faster than restaurants. I consider the two-year run of the *EQRH* remarkable and important" (Moulthrop, interview). Running and contributing to a hypertext journal in pre-web days involved a significant amount of precarious labor, aggravated by brutal market constraints. As Mac speculates, "I expect it was a lot of work to produce. At the time, there wasn't a large market for digital texts; everybody was talking about hypertexts as the evolution of the book, but there weren't many readers. Hypertexts were avant garde novelties, not novels" (interview).

Coinciding factors that contributed to the *EQRH*'s destiny included Eastgate's commercial pricing, which clashed with catering to a niche market when the "ascendancy of the Internet" (Gess, interview) heralded vast popular access to self-publishing online. "The web's ubiquity also removed the element of the exotic from [hypertext] – suddenly breakfast foods were putting up websites that operated on the same technical principles as afternoon, and the genre was no longer thrillingly new" (ibid.).

The niche inhabited by Eastgate limited awareness of serious hypertext to scholars and students. Smyth concedes:

> As a student writing about hypertext in an academic setting,
> I couldn't afford a $50 subscription to the *EQRH*. . . . It was the
> mid-1990s. January 1995 is when color came to the Web; before
> that, it was grey backgrounds. Blue link words and black
> text. . . . The *EQRH* was too ahead of its time, I think; it was
> like the hot dog stand in Ray Bradbury's *The Martian Chronicles*:
> open for business, but no (or too few) customers! (Interview)

The *EQRH*'s subscription model only appealed to very few readers at the
time, who had both material access to the technologies, and an affinity for
nonstandard, on-screen reading practices that evaded notions of closure,
cohesion, plot, and reader control. This small market did not gel well with
Eastgate's disproportionately high production and sales costs:

> They definitely spent some money on that catalogue mailer!
> Two full 16" X 20" pieces of paper, back-to-back color-
> copies . . . that's a lot of overhead! It was a big
> investment, . . . and . . . bug fixes, version updates, etc. all
> required expensive and timely mailing. (Smyth, interview)

In the late 1980s and early 1990s the publishing landscape was highly limited and
fraught with outdated business models. Simultaneously, during those threshold
years evolving screen technologies and computer graphics with their "flickering
signifiers" (Hayles 1993) had not yet developed to an extent that would allow
comfortable on-screen reading experiences. As Cramer explains,

> A lot of discussions of . . . the future of electronic books
> [were ongoing, and] people would spend endless amounts of
> time talking about screen real estate and screen resolution.
> Eastgate . . . had people [who] would buy what it was doing
> in small numbers, and I had a lot of ideas about how Mark
> could do things differently, involving . . . higher-profile
> writers. Higher-profile writers usually had book contracts,
> so you would have to pay them more. . . . There was no
> distribution system . . ., there wasn't the online book sales

> where you could download things and send it [through
> email]. ... And so ... Eastgate was sort of on this island
> of profitability, where if they did what they did, they would
> be okay. And if ... it made any of the obvious changes that
> might have conceivably worked, they would probably fail.
> And so Eastgate has persisted ... remarkably similarly to ...
> where it was when I worked there. ... We could do wild
> things in this particular niche ... but I suspect once the Web
> came in and people started doing much more sort of diffuse,
> anarchic, hypertextual kind of things, there was probably less
> demand for the ... arcane things we were doing. (Interview)

Eastgate's strong auteur identity thus reflected a keen awareness of the risks of changing a brand that reserved them shelter from the rolling waters surrounding its "island of profitability."

Alternative models to Eastgate's serious, text-centered hypertext were pursued by companies like Voyager, which pioneered multimedia and text-commented video LazerDisk and CD-ROM production in the 1980s and early 1990s. According to Douglas, who knew Voyager cofounder Robert Stein, the company "made some money short term" (interview) but had to fold in 1997, less than ten years after its establishment. Its legacy lives on in the history of hypermedia, and yet Stein's resentments and feelings of loss and wasted time (ibid.) are understandable from an entrepreneurial perspective. This is especially pertinent at a time – pre- and post-pandemic – when video has become the prime medium of edutainment. As with Eastgate, both companies might have experienced rapid growth had they been established at a later time and under a more participatory cultural ideology. At least in Eastgate's case, it is of course questionable whether a switch to massification would have been in Bernstein's avant-garde interest.

> Another factor in the waning interest in Eastgate's approach
> to hypertext was that, to many potential readers, the ways in
> which its writing experiments reflected poststructuralist the-
> orems was more interesting to think about than to read. The

> most adroit manipulators of the software, the most inspired
> theorists, were not necessarily equally adept as fiction wri-
> ters. Electronic arts in general are screen arts, a visual
> medium. One reason for the decline in interest may have
> been that lay readers found on-screen constructions of text
> fatiguing and lacking in visual allure. (Gess, interview)

Surely at the time it was not at all clear just how photorealistic screen
technologies would become within a very short time, and at the time, most
PC and Mac users likely saw the technology as a work rather than
entertainment medium.

Many members of the e-literature community have criticized Bernstein's
"reluctance to porting first-gen Eastgate texts to Windows or to 16bit
platforms and beyond" (Joyce, personal correspondence). This is particularly true for Eastgate authors, most of whom cannot access their own
works on current machines. This speaks to an inherent challenge facing
digital culture: the cost associated with creating new media from serious
hypertext to blockbuster video games flies in the face of the ongoing and
costly efforts required to preserve these works and make them accessible to
posterity. And since the free market economy cannot be reasonably
expected to undertake this mammoth task, concerted government, institu-
tionally and charity-funded scholarly undertakings are needed to preserve
the enormous legacy left by pioneer enterprises like Eastgate.

Mark Bernstein frames the *EQRH*'s demise in terms of a dearth of primary
material and a waning interest amongst its main audience, scholars of
postmodernism:

> It might have worked. If we had more hypertexts to work
> with, we might have built a larger base, a larger audience,
> and a larger movement. The question was still, "Where are
> the hypertexts?" It still is. . . . We couldn't pay enough to
> raise eyebrows at the size of our advances. We couldn't
> simply buy audience either. The Web offered an opportu-
> nity to writers to trade their work for celebrity; that

worked, briefly, for a few. A healthy literary economy pays writers.

W eb magazines and anthologies became an important home for short literary hypertext. Carl Steadman's "Suck" created a new link rhetoric. Derek Powazek's "Fray" created a visual style that's still prominent on the Web. Serial web fictions like Kaycee Nicolle, The Spot, and She's A Flight Risk all expanded storytelling in time … HotWired was, for a time, a huge success.

One important challenge the Quarterly faced in the mid-1990s was a critical environment in which postmodernism was increasingly viewed as problematic, and in which we were viewed as postmodernism's progeny. It was safer to call hypertext "claptrap" than to take on Coover or Pynchon, Barthelme or Vonnegut, Barthes or Foucault. … More important, the '90s also saw a reaction against irony and in favor of plot … Literary hypertext had seldom been very interested in plot, and much of its early literature is openly hostile to immersion. (Interview)

The return to the plot went hand in hand with a move away from the kind of networked complexity represented by deeply structured hypertext software like Storyspace. According to Bernstein, "the Web would have been far richer from the start, and it might have been better prepared to withstand the corrupting influence of tyranny and deception" had it been possible to build a foundation with more alternative hypertext models and works during those formative years. The following chapter will illustrate just how "rich" this landscape might have been. It provides analyses of all *EQRH* works to provide a sense of just how innovative, multifaceted, and deeply structured the hypertext writing experiments were that made their way into the *EQRH*.

3 The Works

In this chapter, I undertake a systematic attempt at preservation through traversals. I offer an analytical overview of all works published in the *EQRH*. In some cases, I was able to draw on substantial scholarship while others have received very little or no scholarly attention at all. Figure 4 illustrates *EQRH* scholarship status when I began my research in summer 2018 (Ensslin 2020). The bar chart depicts the results of a combined search of the MLA database, Google Scholar, and Google Books done on June 27, 2018, with duplicate hits removed. Whilst the limited search likely yielded an incomplete picture of the actual research landscape, it allows plausible insights into the *EQRH* works' relative popularity amongst hypertext scholars.

The graph shows an overwhelming preponderance of scholarly references to Douglas's "I Have Said Nothing" and Arnold's "Lust," as well as to Rosenberg's collections. Between one and five mentions referred to Cramer's "In Small & Large Pieces," Falco's "Sea Island," Franco's "Quam Artem Exerceas," Kendall's "A Life Set for Two," Larsen's "Century Cross," Mac's "Unnatural Habitats," and Malin's unpublished yet ostensibly planned "contour and consciousness." Works that have been neglected include Richard Gess's "Mahasukha Halo," Judith Kerman's "Mothering," Richard Smyth's "Genetis: A Rhizography," Rob Swigart's "Directions," and Michael van Mantgem's "Completing the Circle."

The works published in the *EQRH* roughly break into four types, three digital and one paper-based. The creative hypertexts all map across a spectrum between experimental poetry and fiction, and the resulting section headings "Poetry" and "Short Fiction" in this book should be seen as more like poles at the ends of a spectrum than clear-cut genres. After all, all *EQRH* works experiment with the then-new digital medium and explore the breakages with traditional forms they afford. The eight works in the "Poetry" section foreground experimentation with words on screen, image, and sound. They explore the new, medium-specific, spatio-temporal parameters of reading and interacting with language in a way that foregrounds conceptual art over plot. These works include Jim Rosenberg's "Intergrams" (issue 1:1), "The Barrier Frames," and "Diffractions

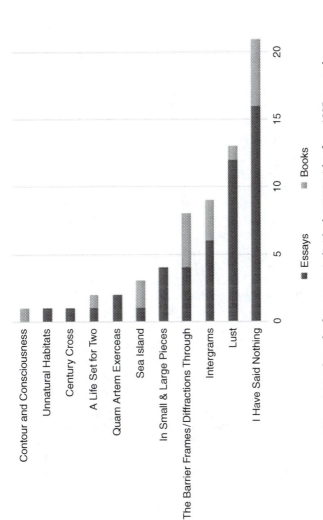

Figure 4 Number of references to individual *EQRH* titles from 1995 onward

Through" (2:3); Kathy Mac's "Unnatural Habitats" (1:3); Rob Swigart's "Directions" (1:4); Edward Falco's "Sea Island" (2:1); Richard Gess's "Mahasukha Halo" (2:1); and Robert Kendall's "A Life Set for Two" (2:4).

The second largest group of works are clustered under "short fiction." Although a clear separation from poetry is in most cases impossible, the short fictions foreground narrativity in the sense of experimentation with delinearized storytelling, plot development, and narrative point of view. These seven works include Mary-Kim Arnold's "Lust" (1:2), J. Yellowlees Douglas's "I Have Said Nothing" (1:2), Kathryn Cramer's "In Small & Large Pieces" (1:3), Judith Kerman's "Mothering" (2:2), Deena Larsen's "Century Cross" (2:2), Michael van Mantgem's "Completing the Circle" (2:2), and Richard Smyth's "Genetis: A Rhizography" (2:4). Kendall's and Smyth's works are the only ones published in the same issue where creative "genres" are mixed (2:4). This may suggest that Bernstein was running out of material from either genre to merit a poetry-only or short-fiction-only issue, thus foreboding the demise of the series. Alternatively, Bernstein may have intended to actively promote a genre-blending agenda, thus reflecting the fluidity of digital textuality and heralding aspects of remix and convergence culture.

EQRH's hypertextual nonfiction comprises only one work: Giuliano Franco's "*Quam Artem Exerceas?*" (1:4). A key reason for the underrepresentation of nonfictional hypertext might be that scholarly and scientific authors like Franco received little support from their institutions for experimental forms of academic publishing. Furthermore, the preponderance of informational hypertext in scientific and encyclopedic treatises like "*Quam Artem*" might already have appeared more suited to the flat HTML structures of the evolving Web 1.0.

Finally, I analyze paratextual print materials that were shipped with the folios. Each issue contained a small booklet with installation and interaction instructions for Windows and Macintosh, author bios, acknowledgments, and individual essays, written either by the authors of the hypertexts published in the same issue, or other eminent scholars. For a more comprehensive understanding of the folios, a multimodal analysis of the cover art, enriched with dedicated interview data from the designers, would have been ideal. However, spatial constraints did not allow me to do so.

3.1 Poetry

The eight hypertext poems differ radically in design and thematic concern, and yet they share a defiance of any standards and reader expectations set by both oral and print culture. They push the limits of meter, rhyme, verse, stanza, syntax, and other vocally and spatially motivated conventions of poetic communication by exploring the spatial and dynamic affordances of the computer screen as a new material platform devoid of the limitations of the page and oral performance. Pre-web hypertext poetry needs the screen to evoke reader interaction via mouse click and mouse-over, and the *EQRH* poets deployed the functionalities of both HyperCard and Storyspace in ways that radically transgressed and artistically reflected on the default affordances of both software packages.

3.1.1 Jim Rosenberg: Folding Visual Language Space

Jim Rosenberg's three poetry cycles, or "stacks," as they may more appropriately be referred to, *Intergrams* (1:1), *The Barrier Frames*, and *Diffractions Through* (2:3), were published in two issues of the *EQRH*, the first and the penultimate one. They therefore have a cyclical and programmatically framing effect on the two volumes. Reading them in their original form requires MacOS 7–9, with HyperCard 2.x or HyperCard Player. Although the poet himself retrospectively sees the *EQRH*-published versions as only temporary snapshots in a long series of developments that have lasted to the present day, they are analyzed here in their historical form, published in the *EQRH* and illustrated with screenshots available from Rosenberg's website (2015).

Rosenberg's poetry subverts the temporal paradigm of reading by mapping poetic language in predominantly spatial terms that eschew sequential decoding and performance. They are experiments in layering semantically dissonant text on individual lexias in HyperCard, in analogy to the chromatic, diatonic, and pentatonic clustering characteristic of John Cage's musical experiments of the 1940s, from which Rosenberg drew inspiration.

Intergrams is a series of eleven works developed from 1988 and 1992, thus predating the *EQRH* by half a decade. Ultimately, the series dates back to

Rosenberg's first experiments with diagrammatic formats (*Diagram Poems*) in the late 1960s. *Intergrams* does not aim at semantic coherence or memetic-imaginary comprehension in the reader. Instead, it is driven by the idea of using hypertext as a "medium of thought" (Rosenberg 1996), foregrounding and subverting syntactic structures that usually remain implicit in poetic and everyday language. The work is an extensive experiment with possibilities of "asyntactic poetry" that are characterized by simultaneity and complex, multilayered stacking and clustering. Inspired by Cage's tonal clusters and musical "null relationships" (Rosenberg 1996: 104), Rosenberg sought to develop an "explicit structural vocabulary" (ibid.) that demarcates hierarchical relationships between clusters, such as quasi-verb and quasi-complement dependencies, yet at the same time defunctionalizing them in a communicative-pragmatic sense.

In terms of user interaction, the poems are "technically speaking completely static. As you move the mouse, the screen changes by bringing different 'cards' to the front (or navigating to them, in the original version). There is no actual algorithmic changing of text" (Rosenberg, interview). Thus the pieces cannot be performed in the form of a traversal, and interaction with them feels more like inspecting the layers of an assortment of intricately composed palimpsests, or the individual notes in a series of multilayered musical chords that only allow fleeting glimpses into their composite parts before they conflate again into semi-impermeable arrays of leveled language (see Figure 5). Rosenberg himself describes natural language as "a *FOLDED* linear space; the function of syntax is to introduce embedded storage cues for how the folding and unfolding works … The computer [by contrast] allows folded linear space to be replaced by networked visual interactive space in which the folding and unfolding are made physical by the action of the reader, nonlinearly, unconstrained by synchronized time" (interview).

In the introductory sequence of lexias, Rosenberg explains the operational principles of *Intergrams* thus:

> Each poem consists of several screens. On each screen will be various word clusters. A word cluster is a group of phrases that all occupy the same point in space, physically

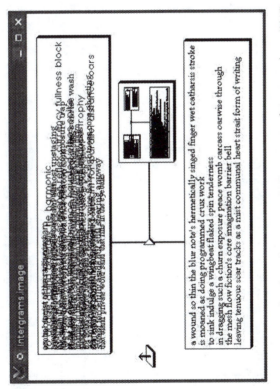

Figure 5 Screenshot from "Intergrams 11." Courtesy of Jim Rosenberg (2015)

> and logically. The phrases in the word cluster are meant to
> be juxtaposed with no structural relationships between them,
> and the word cluster is meant to be read as the juxtaposition
> of all of its phrases. When you first view a screen, all of the
> phrases in a word cluster will appear on top of one another –
> most likely making nearly all the words illegible. By moving
> the mouse you can make each individual phrase in the
> cluster appear all by itself, so that it becomes (temporarily)
> readable. For each phrase there is a rectangular area where
> whenever the cursor is in this area the phrase becomes
> visible.

In another introductory lexia, Rosenberg stresses that "[b]ecause the phrases of a cluster occur in the same space, they must not be constrained in time" and are therefore unperformable. Each Intergram displays a different constellation of hierarchical tree relationships, and the phrases and words in the clusters are assembled in a way that prevents readers from construing any logical or other meaningful semantic connections between them. Rosenberg (1994) calls this principle a "non-linear, non-link structuring method." It lends *Intergrams* a strong, almost excessively aleatoric feel, similar to contemporary bot poetry yet undermining the probabilistic potential of bot poetry to generate meaningful conjunctions. The fact that the lexical and phraseological units in the clusters were manually composed rather than computationally generated makes Intergrams a prime example of proto-bot poetry (Ensslin 2019).

The Barrier Frames and *Diffractions Through*, published in issue 2:3, are two further poetic experiments that evolve from *Intergrams*, thus lending a non-completist sense of closure to the prematurely folded periodical publication. On his website, Rosenberg (2015) offers multi-platform versions of each work for download. *Diffractions Through*, which appears alphabetically before *The Barrier Frames*, was inspired by John Cage's death. It

> transformed the writing of this piece; I might perhaps have
> called it Re and Not Re John Cage. At that time I found

> myself repeating a phrase that other friends also found
> helpful: "John Cage: Not in memoriam but in use, in con-
> tinuous use." This work represents an infinitesimal fragment
> of that continuous use. (Rosenberg 2015)

The notion of "continuous use" is evoked strongly when interacting with the work. Reading the individual elements in the stack unravels Rosenberg's "polylinear 'word nets' and subdiagrams" (Rosenberg 2015) (see Figure 6). They are conceptualized as alternatives to regular, hypertextual multilinearity that leads to sequentialization of action and plot.

The Barrier Frames (Figure 7) contains nine "densely layered 'nested' simultaneities." Rosenberg (2015) transgresses hypertextual multilinearity even further by introducing an "almost pure spatial hypertext" that visualizes Rosenberg's tonal clustering effect most holistically. "This simultaneity, or 'equivalenced time,' is an abstraction that the reader must just infer" (ibid.) because it clashes with our human understanding of language as a temporally sequenced perceptive effect.

Each cluster consists of multiple embedded objects that appear as a densely layered cloud of words on the entry screen. Upon mouse-over, individual, random frames from the layers of the cluster pop up on the screen, either displaying one layer of text only or clusters within clusters. As the reader moves the mouse along the edges of each frame, they appear or disappear, depending on which frame has been thus activated. This lends the experience of the work a dynamic sense of reading that is, however, not generative in style and retains reader agency despite the semantic elusiveness of the *texte-à-voir*.

From a technical perspective, Rosenberg was inspired by HyperCard's mouse-over functionality that saved him an extensive amount of Smalltalk programming. At the same time, "there is no text here" (CDS, Brown University 1999) in the sense that each textual object is essentially a computer graphic. This gives the author a significant amount of control over fonts and other error-prone features of text processing. On the whole, however, assembling his diagrammatic works by hand was an excessively "laborious" effort, with the scripting of on-screen language only taking up about 5 percent of the entire compositional process. Ninety-five percent of

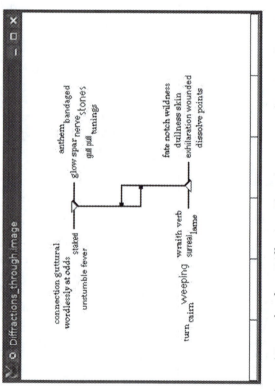

Figure 6 Screenshot from *Diffractions Through*. Courtesy of Jim Rosenberg (2015)

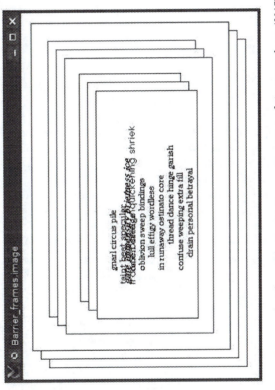

Figure 7 Screenshot from *The Barrier Frames*. Courtesy of Jim Rosenberg (2015)

Rosenberg's time thus went into constructing the layered infrastructure of his works (CDS, Brown University 1999).

In terms of folio and cover design, *Intergrams* came in a simple, black vinyl folio imprinted with golden letters. Upon aging, vinyl has the adverse effect of making pages stick to it. The copy I was using at the ELL is therefore even more prone to wear and tear than the cardboard jackets introduced later by Eastgate. Preserving the vinyl editions in material and scholarly form is thus even more challenging and urgent than preserving the cardboard ones.

3.1.2 "Into an Alien Ocean": Kathy Mac's "Unnatural Habitats"

In her poetic pastiche, "Unnatural Habitats" (UH), Canadian writer and scholar Kathleen McConnell, alias Kathy Mac, appeared in issue 1:3 (1994) of the *EQRH*, alongside Kathryn Cramer's "In Small and Large Pieces" (see 3.2.3). It has 96 writing spaces and 288 links, with a file size of 207.9 k. The work explores the spatial affordances of Storyspace hypertext both formally and thematically. It engages with the ways in which modernity's phallogocentric strife for teleological technological progress and masculine dominance has created numerous subjugating, alienating and potentially fatal spaces for humans and other animals.

The work is an intricately interlinked cycle of poems, divided into twelve individual paths (see Figure 8), the first six of which represent habitats that are physically and physiologically unnatural for humans like space, the deep sea, and the desert. The second tier, comprising four poems, revolves around conceptual unnatural habitats like religious and other types of cultural differences. The two poems in the third tier remix elements of the two top tiers. Strikingly, the individual paths, arranged in the form of a visual cycle around the contents space (Figure 8), do not directly map onto twelve independent habitats. For example, the two across the top ("Apollo 13: Reentry" and "Apollo 13: Interface") quite literally interface and leave the reader looping between them whilst revolving around the same poetic material, the failed Apollo 13 mission in 1970. Similarly, the two paths across the bottom are composed of individual fragments of other paths, thus generating a summative intertextual quilt representing a "blanket made out of pieces."

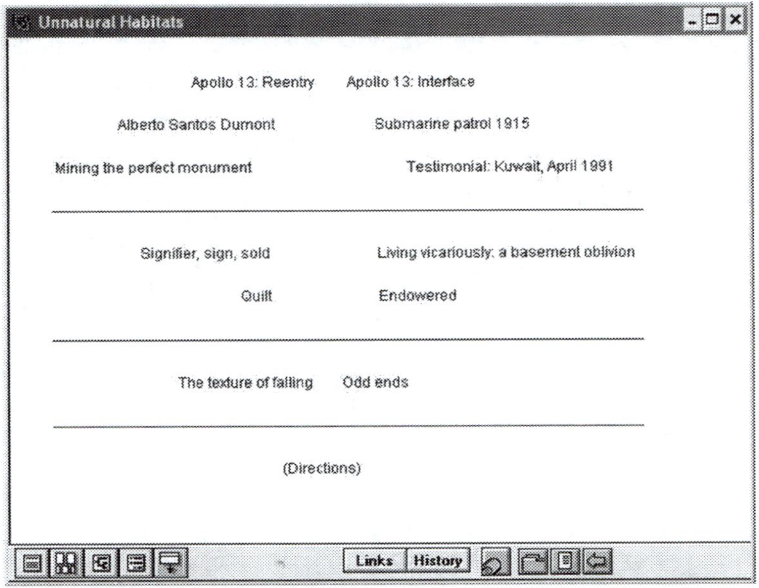

Figure 8 UH, contents page (Oracle VM Virtualbox)

A painting dolphin is the protagonist in the "Signifier, sign, sold" path. Its plight is to be imprisoned "in a pool somewhere on the prairies" whilst not being able to exist in the wild, "alien ocean." The text's focus on animal rights is an important addition to the "women and men" whose physically and socially unnatural habitats are exemplified by notions of outer space, air travel ("Alberto Santos Dumont"), "Submarine Patrol," modern warfare ("Testimonial Kuwait, April 1991"), Islamic marital laws (viewed from a Western, feminist perspective in "Endowered"), and even the virtual spaces mediated by computer screens ("Living vicariously: a basement oblivion"). Thus, whilst the specific unnatural habitats chosen by Mac may seem "eclectic" (Mac's letter to Mark Bernstein, early June 1993), they jointly contribute to the text's critique of capitalist exploitation and UH's significance as an early digital work of literary ecofeminism.

Following in the footsteps of visual and concrete poetry, UH exploits the spatial constraints of a lexia window for textual positioning and perceived movement. It places short poetic segments, or stanzas, in various places on the screen, forming either upward or downward movements when read according to the default paths. For example, the "Alberto Santos Dumont" section describes an ascending and subsequently descending movement in the default reading path, thus depicting the take-off and landing of an aeroplane or, on a more abstract level, the rise and fall of Dumont's health and achievements as an early twentieth-century aeronautic pioneer. By contrast, the "Submarine Patrol 1915" path describes an overall downward movement, but it also suggests, via Storyspace's "Navigation" functionality, that readers move to the Dumont pathway after finishing the final lexia, "Sub: border."

Mac's primary goal with UH was to explore how the digital medium might help writers subvert analog traditions of beginning, middle, and end, as well as move beyond words on a page:

> A lot of "Unnatural Habitats" is not about the words themselves, but about weaving the lines between the text-blocks together in different shapes – the negative spaces of the stories. ... I don't know of any other hypertext that

> concerned itself with that, and that concern was really only
> possible with Storyspace. (Interview)

Her emphasis on the spaces and links between individual words and lexias is reminiscent of Jim Rosenberg's spatial hypertext. However, whilst Rosenberg's intent lies in nesting and stacking lexias into diagrammatic structures that defy human temporal decoding and narrativization, Mac's approach is distinctly linear and intertextually meaningful. It led to a variety of linking structures in and between individual pathways in UH, and to different visualizations of these structures and their connections to thematic issues of the poems in each segment's map view. The "Signifier, sign, sold" path, for example, outlines a zigzag pattern to represent the waves engulfing a dolphin in natural waters, "Testimonial Kuwait" displays a star of the American flag, and the "Weftfork" in the third, remix tier describes the movement of shuttle in a loom (see Grigar et al. 2021).

The weaving metaphor runs through the entire work, reflecting Mac's deep interest in the relationship between text and textile. Mac's PhD was about textile metaphors in the literature of the Industrial Revolution, and Storyspace allowed her to combine and entextualize formal elements of weaving, such as interlacing, repetition, patterning, and cyclicality. Cyclicality is also found in the parallelism between the unidirectional loop of the two Apollo 13 paths and the second tier of the work, where readers cycle unidirectionally between, "Living vicariously," "Endowered," and "Quilt." Although this moves them between seemingly disconnected story-worlds such as that of a dolphin in a show aquarium, a computer addict in a basement, situations of domestic abuse in Islamic culture, and the repatching of an army uniform into an AIDS quilt, the cycle has internal cohesion afforded by the theme of unnatural lived and textual spaces. The final and bottom section of UH then picks up the theme of text as an interwoven structure. "The texture of falling" begins with a definition of "TEXT" as "woven; also fabric, structure, from 'texere,' to weave," exposing textuality as "Just a blanket made out of pieces." This path again dissipates into fragments of lexias visited in other sections of the work and ends with the final lexia from "Apollo 13: Reentry," thus adding a sense of closure to the work. The final lexia in this path ("13-Reentry/Fall") reiterates the material ambivalence between outer space and represented, textual space, and underscores the liminality of spaces between natural and unnatural habitats, perceived as both "noise" and "silence" (Figure 9). The spatially separated period following the tapering end stanza further materializes and visualizes the end of this path and the text as a whole.

In her 1993 correspondence with Bernstein, Mac details the challenges facing her in creating dynamic links and guard fields for UH. Dynamic, unidirectional links are "a distinctive feature of Storyspace ... that can be activated or deactivated by ... guard field[s]" (Bernstein 2016: 2). Guard fields are Boolean expressions that change a reader's path according to lexias they have or haven't visited before, thus "prov[ing] invaluable for breaking cycles" (ibid.), or infinite loops, in a hypertext reading. In an email to Bernstein of early June 1993, Mac describes her "technical frustrations" in trying to create links between paths:

> This hypertext consists of several discreet paths, and two paths (named "mingle" and "gravity") which cross the other paths at will. My main problem is that some of my text spaces are common to two paths. I haven't figured out yet how to tell Storyspace that when a reader comes from box A which is on path 1, the default path is path 1, but if the reader comes from box z along path 2, the default path is path 2. I'm hoping that there is some magic way of scripting this in the guard fields, but as yet, the best I can manage is to bring the reading process to a dead halt at the intersecting box, and force the reader to look up the links and choose one.

These "dead halts" between intersecting paths happen throughout UH. Although they were Mac's "hardly elegant" (letter to Bernstein, July 27, 1993) response to not being able to modify guard fields as she intended, the dead halts can be considered a key aesthetic feature of the reading experience – one that draws the reader's attention to the ways in which individual paths are interconnected and form various types of movement – undulating, cyclical, and dissipating.

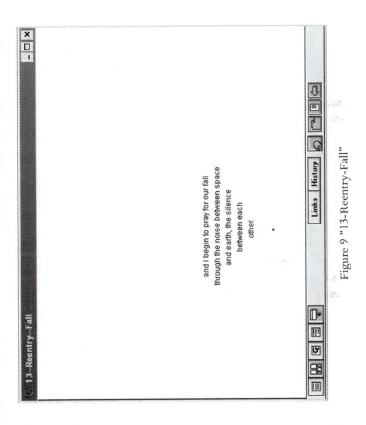

Figure 9 "13–Reentry–Fall"

Another question Mac sought help with in her 1993 correspondence with Bernstein was in relation to the "Endowered" path, which focuses on Islamic law and the rights of women as set forth in the Quran. Concerned about her status as non-Islamic author critiquing Islamic law, Mac worried, "The path I have taken is somewhat inflammatory, especially considering that I am not a Moslem ... injustice is injustice. On the other hand, the situation in the former Yugoslavia is divided along Christian/Moslem lines, and I don't want to sound like a cultural elitist." In a later letter, Mac responds to undocumented advice she received from Bernstein shortly afterward, both on "Endowered" and the guard field issue:

> [T]hank you for your advice re: the Endowered path; you've helped me pinpoint the problems that I felt were there, but which I couldn't quite put my finger on. I had thought that it was too inflammatory, but perhaps the real problem was that it was too boring. ... Thanks for your advice about guard fields. I do have a copy of Getting Started with Storyspace, but find that the directions are sometimes a bit obtuse.

At the time Mac worked with me on this project, and on a public traversal of UH in spring 2021 (Grigar et al. 2021a), she had revoked the "Endowered" path completely and excluded it from her public performance of the work.

In the same 1993 correspondence with Bernstein, Mac also mentions the SuperPaint file (an early graphics editing software developed by Richard Shoup at Xerox PARC) in which the title screen was designed (Figure 10). The design is not printed on the folio and has thus been concealed from public and scholarly view. The screen is a collage of pixelated, flowery shapes on the left, set against a woven, cross-hatching texture. Both images were photocopies of scarves, arranged in such a way as to show the contrasts between the curvilinear, spiral shapes of the flowers on the left with the warp-and-wefty pattern on the right. The title text is formatted so as to change from italics to sans serif bold and back. These conceptual and aesthetic clashes echo the theme of the work, foregrounding alienation and experimental textuality. They also reflect the fact that Mac was working

Figure 10 UH, title page

with nineteenth-century movable type in a typography course she took at the same time as writing UH.

According to her correspondence with Bernstein, Mac intended to incorporate "more visual bells-and-whistles" in the Storyspace work, yet finally gave in to Storyspace's limited capacity for visual graphics and other non-textual features.

3.1.3 "The Shattered Eye Sees Deeper": Rob Swigart's "Directions"

"Directions" by futurist writer and emeritus professor of English Rob Swigart is an extended, "quasi-sentimental pseudo-scientific hyperpoem" (Swigart 1994) made in HyperCard and readable on historical Macintosh machines running System 7. The work, which is strictly speaking a cycle of hyperpoems, was originally published in issue 1:4 of the *EQRH*, along with Giuliano Franco's "*Quam Artem Exerceas?*" (3.3). This material co-situatedness is not coincidental, as both works represent experimental approaches to hypertextualizing scientific historiography. Yet their formal aesthetics differ radically: whilst Franco follows a scholarly, informational hypertextual model of maximum structural and semantic clarity and logical coherence, Swigart adopts a radically dissonant, albeit affectively cohesive poetic agenda.

"Directions" poetically and multimodally explores questions of relative directionality, of elusive beginnings and endings, of possible paths and impossible destinations. It takes hypertext linking and navigation to an expressive and experiential extreme. The work features a diversity of semiotic modes and textual genres, including astronomical images, scientific graphs and maps, poetic fragments, philosophical and anthropological scholarly prose, black-and-white BITMAP images, and diverse sound effects. Readers start from and keep returning to a stylistically and poetically adapted periodic table of elements. This central navigational node is called "Elemental Table of Directions," and its design reflects the historical status quo of chemistry in the mid-1990s, when elements 107–118 were still undefined and therefore missing from the table (Figure 11). Each element in the table is linked to a text/image lexia that takes readers on an indefinitely looping, occasionally multilinear journey through the cycle.

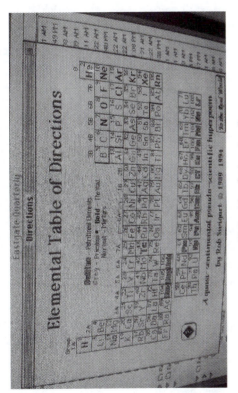

Figure 11 "Table of Directions"

Each text-image BITMAP reads as an inherently meaningful multimodal cluster, and the reading process becomes a performance of the core thematic concern of the text: the tension between cyclicality and teleology in human orientation and existence.

As shown in Figure 11, the chemical elements are formatted differently, so as to match the diversely formatted words in the stylized key right above the table. The key contains the words "Outline," "Patrilineal Elements," "Grey," "Priestess," "Bold," "TheVoid," "Normal," and "Martyrs." In my own traversals, I consistently failed to read a consistent navigational meaning into these clustered formattings. As Swigart explained in his interview, the original intent behind this visual design was an even more complex symbolical-navigational system, which nonetheless turned out to be unfeasible given the time constraints facing his project.

Swigart's graphic images involve symbolic and geometric shapes and diagrams, ethnological objects, desert landscapes, waves, and an animated Greek column that readers can destroy and/or erect as a "consequence of failure" or "success" respectively. A bird's-eye view of an archeological site has a text box displayed above it, which runs animated text inserted by the reader via a text box – a unique, platform-specific feature offered by HyperCard at the time. Perhaps the most powerful, linear sequence of image–text lexias depicts a large eye looking directly at the reader accompanied by the text, "The mirror, widened, defeats loss." Upon repeated clicking, the eye gradually becomes larger, breaking apart along the center. The text under the final, split eye reads, "The shattered eye sees deeper, without deceit" (Figure 12). The image–text combination thus suggests a rhetorical metalepsis – that is, "a small window that allows a quick glance across the fictional and the actual world" (Ryan 2006: 207) – between the poetic agent, represented by the eye, and the reader, who is led to feel addressed by the eye, and to seek comprehension and transparent directionality beyond the sensorily intelligible.

Recurring themes include death and decay, starvation, injury, pain, and other aspects of human loss, suffering, uncertainty, and destruction. Yet there is also a strong counternarrative of cyclicality and rebirth, which is paralleled by the reader's looping movement through the hypertext. Despite the absence of any clearly intelligible characters or voices, in some reading

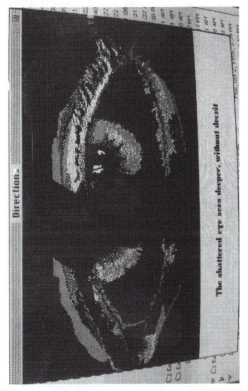

Figure 12 "The shattered eye"

paths, figures of a priest and priestess occur, framed in an ancient Egyptian fertility myth that evokes rebirth out of lost memory, "beginning with death." Another key parallel between content and form is the idea of directionality in navigation. A nodal lexia, which branches into five, one-lexia sub-paths, reads, "Direction is neither casual nor easily known . . . / Yet it is as always, indirect" (Figure 13). The rhetorical figure of kyklos evoked by the reiteration of "direct" ("direction . . . indirect") appears in morphologically adapted and semantically reversed form, thus undermining its own potentiality for absolute closure. The lexia thus epitomizes the way in which "Directions" thematizes, through diverse textual, procedural, and multimodal constellations, the deconstruction of straightforward, mono-linear navigation in a dated, teleologically oriented world picture that is in the process of departing and deviating from established, arborescent, logo-centric, and unidirectional structures.

This anti-logocentrism is further augmented by an abundance of sound effects throughout the poem. Clicking hyperlinks in the work often triggers auditive explosions, blast-offs, and gongs, but also more esoteric, seemingly extraterrestrial sounds connoting metaphysical transcendence and a bridging of ontological spheres that are incomprehensible through con-ventional, linear human communication. Furthermore, when read on 1990s Macintosh, the sound becomes haptic: the integrated speakers make the entire hardware resonate with the sound, augmenting the metaleptic, world-transcending effects of the image–text on screen.

The link "To the Real World" in the bottom right corner of the entry lexia offers readers a figurative way out of the fictional universe of the poem and into the actual world of the reader. Readers can close the program by making a binary decision on the following, final lexia, "Elementary parti-cles," where they can choose between "Yes, I want to go back to the Real World," and "No, I don't want to leave these wonders." The former will figuratively catapult readers out of the poem's universe of elementary, transcendent particles, accompanied by a loud, explosive noise. The latter will return them to the periodic table as the work's primary, atomic orientation device that maps Swigart's poetic universe of "peripheries" onto its "elemental" essence. On his website, Swigart (2020) comments on the evanescence of his work:

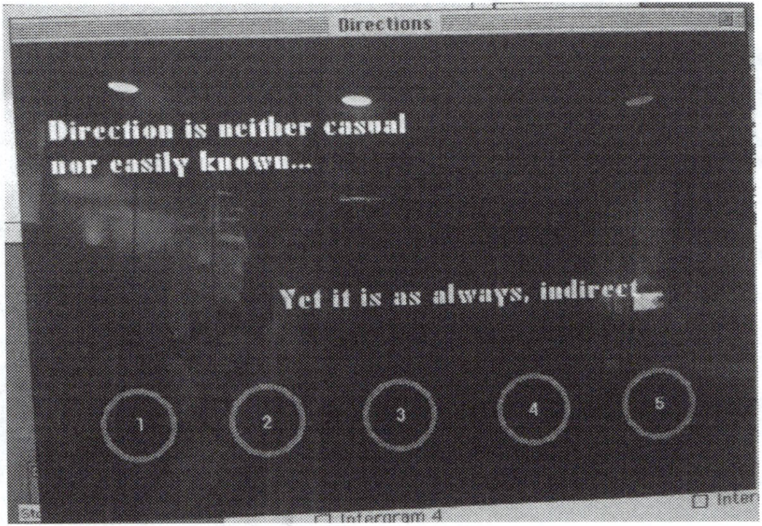

Figure 13 Screenshot from Swigart's *Directions*

> Unfortunately bit-rot has set in and Hypercard is no longer
> a viable platform, so Directions has gone the way of the
> pterosaur. ... This is the price of progress. We may be
> encouraged, though, that some art is meant to be evanes-
> cent, and to fade away without a trace.

Evidently, "Directions" has all but "faded away" more than two decades after
its genesis. It may not be as well known as many other pre-web hypertexts,
but it remains fully readable on historical machines. Similarly, the ways in
which the work's design, thematic concern, and hypertextual expressivity
testify to a specific and key historical moment in the history of science and
technology is symptomatic of the need for its preservation. Swigart chose to
publish his work in a periodical that was stored and disseminated on data
carriers. This does invoke the intent of preservation, at least temporarily.

In relation to his motivations behind the content and design of
"Directions," Swigart explains that, as a non-programmer, he was inspired
by the technological possibilities HyperCard offered to artists and writers
without a strong technical background. In the first instance, this inspiration
came about during a writing workshop in the 1990s with Yale Younger poet
William Dickey:

> We were both interested in Hypercard as a medium for
> creating poetry in particular. ... Hypercard made it possible
> for individuals to create in this new medium. There were
> very few places where such work could get published.
> Unfortunately Bill, who died in 1994, never got to see his
> work in published form. It's too bad, because he was brilliant.

HyperCard became "an extremely valuable tool" for Swigart: "I haven't
found one that good since. Various hypertext platforms have emerged and
submerged. ... I would only say that I had a lot of fun and learned
interesting things." Similarly, for Swigart, "Directions" was

> a way of experimenting with features of the program like
> graphic and sound ... I would say the original intention was

> play, see what effects it could make, how it put text, image
> and sound together in surprising ways. (Interview)

For Swigart, then, Eastgate's entrepreneurialism came at an apt time. The publisher "was fairly genial in those days, and the quarterly looked and felt like a legitimate literary venue. I was happy Directions found a home there" (interview). Furthermore, Swigart felt encouraged by Bernstein's hands-off approach, which involved "no real interference with the creative process." The flipside of this was the almost complete absence of editorial or technical support, coupled with the difficulty "to find ways to prolong the life of Eastgate works," which led Swigart to eventually abandon his links with the publishing house.

3.1.4 "What's in Here out There": Edward Falco's *Sea Island*

Virginia-based American writer Edward Falco's work has spanned numerous genres and platforms, and whilst he is arguably best known for his print novels, his significance for the genesis and development of e-literature cannot be underestimated. His well-known 1997 Eastgate hypertext novel, *A Dream with Demons*, remains under-researched, yet his contribution to e-literature publishing has had a lasting effect on the community. In 1996 he founded the online literary journal *The New River*, which has remained a seminal platform for writers of e-literature to the present day and can be seen as "an Internet-age successor" (Falco, interview) to the *EQRH*.

Falco's *Sea Island: hypertext poems* is a cycle of ten short lyrical works created in Storyspace and published in *EQRH* 2:1. It comprises 221 spaces and 1,039 links. The poems are titled "Sea Island," "Summer Flowers," "The Crazy Sea of Language," "Out Here," "Five Women in a Bed," "God Bless the Child," "One Line of Sunlight Pierces," "In This That Just Is," "Passion's," and "Casting Out." As shown in Figure 14, the contents page is arranged in three vertical columns, with two further sections, "Acknowledgments" and "About Reading," across the bottom.

In the "About Reading" lexia, dated January 31, 1995, Falco explains that the poems can be read via their default paths by pressing "Return," by double-clicking on any linked words in the lexias, or via the link navigation browser. "Any combination of the three methods will also work," and Falco

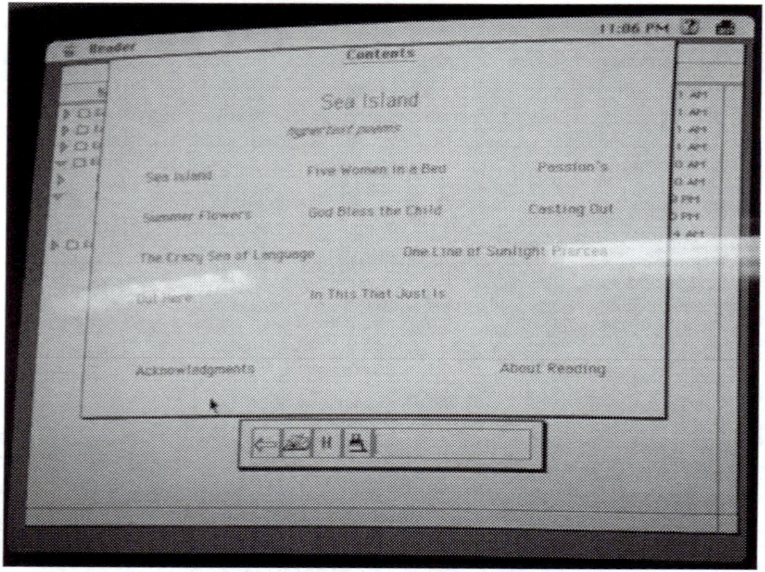

Figure 14 Contents page of *Sea Island*

observes that "[b]ecause hypertext poetry is something new, there is not yet a body of literature prescribing preferred methods of reading. Pretty much you're on your own." This suggests that, in the mid-1990s there was an expectation at least amongst some hypertext writers that prescriptive rather than descriptive scholarship would emerge sooner or later, which would set the standards for reading and analyzing texts in this medium. In hindsight, this turned out to be a misconception as scholars have come to agree that literary hypertext defies standardization and that the Storyspace School remained experimental and defamiliarizing in its endeavor to explore new ways of reading and writing.

In "Acknowledgments" we learn that some of the poems were previously published in the form of their default paths in literary print and online journals: "Out Here," "Sea Island," and "Summer Flowers" in the online journal *BluePenny Quarterly*, "God Bless the Child" in *The Hayden's Ferry Review*, "Five Women in a Bed" in *Quarterly West*, and "Casting Out" in *The Western Humanities Review*. This remediation provides a sense of cross-platform continuity and demonstrates Bernstein's willingness to experiment with copyright implications.

As indicated by the thematic title of the cycle, many of its poems revolve around aquatic or maritime themes and concepts. In my traversal I read them from left to right and top to bottom as reflected in the contents list, first following the default reading path and then clicking on random words in each lexia for a more mashed-up, open-ended effect. The end of each default path, when read on a Macintosh Performa 5215 CD, was marked with a sharp beep from the computer's sound card, which amplified the haptic experience of not getting a system response to any further attempts at pressing the Return key.

"Sea Island," the first poem in the cycle, displays short fragments of impressionistic memories. Each stanzaic lexia spans between one and seven lines, and there are twenty stanzas in total. The poem relates a seaside holiday of the speaker's family and that of a friend, with their children. The sea is described as forceful and threatening, and illusion blends with the realism of actual experience ("What's in here out there"), manifesting in the motives of "An alligator in the surf / A deer / A dying woman." The closing line, "One time," both describes the suddenness of a flash of lightning and the fleetingness of the memory itself, invoking a sense of awe, melancholy and loss.

"Five Women in a Bed" (sixteen stanzas, one to six verses each) is told from the perspective of a man, narrated in first and third person, who, prompted by a photograph of "two red blouses, a blue / Skirt, shoes, curve of leg, curve of thigh" recalls an event at a party, where five women "jump on their host's bed," a moment of ecstatic fun that the speaker witnessed yet felt excluded from ("Outside the picture"). The event may have happened in the speaker's youth, or at some other stage in his life that left him feeling socially awkward, isolated, judgmental, and jealous at the same time ("Women, not the idea of women"; "he wanted / To crawl into their arms and be comforted"). The party imagery is mapped onto that of a lifeboat that "He is swimming hard toward," trying to catch up. Again, there are five women in the boat, and the nautic imagery reinforces the sense of social and emotional despair experienced by the speaker, whose feelings and gazes are experienced as alienating by the women objectified by his gaze ("This guy had this look like this look in his eyes like, this look").

"Passion's" (twenty-eight stanzas, one to five verses each) thematizes disconnect with the speaker's body and soul following parental abuse ("Father his fist is night"; "The impact deepest in the body / The way it learns inadequacy"). The water theme is only marginally touched upon, in relation to fluids inside and outside the alienated body ("Body's water / Blood and tears"; "Steps out of the bath the foreign body / That lives beneath familiar clothes"). The stream of consciousness in the poem becomes more and more diffuse and asyntactic as the linear path progresses, and the speaker's sense of dysphoria is reflected in the poem's apostrophic title, where the genitive lacks a syntactic complement.

In "Summer Flowers" (twenty-two stanzas, one to six verses each), the speaker recalls a love affair with a friend's wife, forty years before writing. He reflects on a moment when the two lovers spent time together in a riverbed, "[o]n an island where we stopped to gather flowers." The water theme assumes romantic, erotic connotations, underscoring the forbidden yet playful bliss experienced by the couple before "some ugliness between me and my friend" ended the affair.

"God bless the Child" (ten lexias of four to twelve lines) presents a musing speaker's ongoing stream of consciousness, clustering asyndetic fragments of childhood memories together into a fast-moving flow of loosely connected phrases in open-ended syntax. The poem is modeled "after Eric Dolphy," a mid-twentieth-century jazz musician known for his improvisational style, and dedicated to a person named Frank. It takes the form of a dialogue between the reminiscing speaker and a much older brother, addressed in the second person. Biographical information about the brother's vinyl collection, his car, and his studies at the "School of Music and Art" gives the poem a distinctly eulogic character, and it mentions their parents and a mysterious person referred to as "she" – possibly an unrequited love of either one of the two siblings.

With its extremely short stanzas, "Casting Out" (twenty-eight lexias of one to four lines) forms a counterpoint to "God Bless the Child." It presents a speaker's thoughts as they are drifting from a more pastoral, idyllic setting ("A pair of bees / Yellow jackets / Buzzing around a cow") surrounding a "teenage boy in jeans and a T-shirt," "through water" to a more disruptive ("Cast out spun away"; "ripped away and cast"), dark, "real world" setting "under deep water." The water theme thus adopts a transitional and threatening tone, echoing the poem's title in the sense of a loss of innocence and perceived security.

Dedicated to feminist scholar and poet Ruth Salvaggio, "The Crazy Sea of Language" (twelve lexias of one to five lines) deploys aquatic imagery to describe the speaker's and his muse's shared writerly destiny ("We all swim in the same crazy sea / We are all always under water"). It addresses Salvaggio in the second person ("You with a mug of coffee at your desk / Composed of and composing"), echoing her feminist work on rereading poetic language in an anti-phallogocentric, aurally inclined subjectivity ("On the other end nouns call for the I") and framing her as a friend or close interlocutor.

"One Line of Sunlight Pierces" (twenty-two lexias of mostly one-line or one-word stanzas) is a short, meditative poetic sketch that addresses a person – possibly the speaker themself – whose isolation in a "dark room" is "pierced through" by a ray of sunlight. The contrasts between darkness and light instill a sense of hope and safety, and sparsity of words on each lexia ("Deep"; "Light") evokes an almost hypnotic sense of calm and self-centering. Thus, the island theme is taken out of its maritime context and projected onto a metaphysical, psychological level, centering self-soothing, subjectivity and mindfulness.

"Out Here" (twenty-two lexias, one to five lines) deals with the concepts of war, destruction, and loss. It projects two individuals who have sought shelter from their "shelled cities" in the wake of the first Gulf War. The poem's opening scene projects them on a dirt road, "Cratered by weather / Crossed six times by shallow creeks." The soothing distance to the war-torn city is evoked by the "popular tune" of "shallow water / Over rocks in a creek bed." The rural countryside becomes the programmatic, metaphorical island that offers "calm" and shelter from the "wreckage" and "panic."

The last poem in the cycle, "In This That Just Is" (twenty-one lexias of mostly single lines of words), is the most fragmented and cryptic. It interweaves meteorological, astronomic, geological, and haptic concepts suggesting different degrees of liquidity ("Star Rain," "Body Juicy Sticky," "Earth / In This Heat") into an existentialist array of ontological absolutes such as "Dark Is," "Space Is," and the titular "In This That Just Is." The closure one might expect from a final poem in a cycle is thus eluded, which is only apt in a hypertext poetry cycle that encourages readers to criss-cross its material in a personalized trajectory. The sheer ideas of cyclicality and finality are thus called into question in a hypertext environment.

Another unique hypertextual technique deployed by Falco is poetic linking. The "Writing Spaces" readers can access in Storyspace shows how Falco embedded poetry in the hyperlinks themselves, thus adding a lyrical, meditative quality to navigation itself and constructing a metapoetic layer (Figure 15). Falco thus exploits the idea of a writing space, both in the diegetic worlds of the poems themselves and in the extra- and metadiegetic space of navigation.

3.1.5 "Iron Weights Swinging from Their Pricks": Richard Gess's "Mahasukha Halo"

"Mahasukha Halo" (MH) is a short, poetic-meditative Storyspace hypertext by North Carolina poet and writer Richard Gess in issue no. 2:1 of the

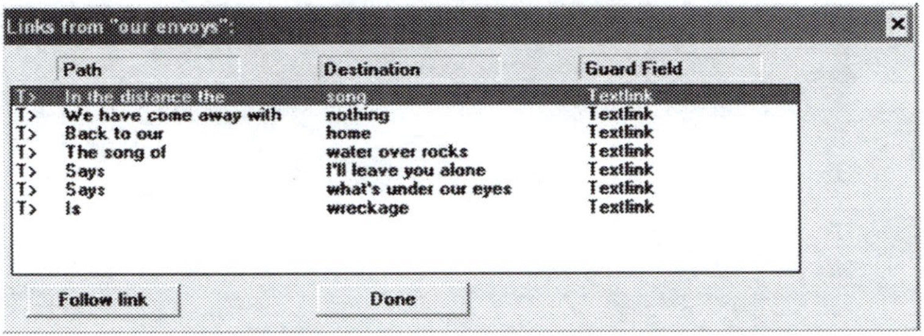

Figure 15 Poetic linking in *Sea Island*

EQRH. It comprises 308 text spaces and 759 links. "Mahasukha" refers to the "Nepalese Buddhist concept of transcendence through erotic experience" (Eastgate Systems 1995), and "Halo" designates the cloudlike structure in which the lexias and reading paths are arranged in the hypertext overview map. The poetic narrative itself implements these ideas by taking the reader through a randomly traversed, materially obfuscating sequence of lexias referencing sexual and death rituals from a foreign, otherworldly culture that remains indistinct throughout yet makes itself felt with visceral intensity.

In line with Stan Brakhage's architectonic films, MH reads like a "succession of images that do not tell a story but define a state of mind" (Davenport 1981: 317) and is meant as a "field of images for interactive exploration" (Gess 1993: 257). From the first lexia titled "Step," readers choose between "up" and "down" (Figure 16). These bidirectional links may indicate parallel universes, or access to the over and underworld, yet the full meaning of these positional opposites remains largely tentative. Depending on the lexias visited, readers undergo a dreamlike or nightmarish experience that leaves the work's narrative voices hard to identify. As Gess (1993) explains, "[s]entences with the same speaker [such as 'Lay Contractor,' 'Lost Missionary,' and 'Athelstan Spilhaus'] or subject [such as 'Sky'] are linked in circular paths, as are sentences sharing images or comprising partial narratives" (257). All lexias and circular paths are equally weighted and can be mutually transgressed, and the interweaving of narratively equivalent paths, as well as the ways in which the narrative fragments, repeats, loops, and digresses, are aimed to make the reader "feel lost [in hyperspace]" (Gess 1993: 257; Conklin 1987).

Many lexias in MH revolve around male sexual organs and phallocentric, ritualistic religiousness ("cat penis," "women with pointing penis noses," "iron weights swinging from their pricks"). Other motifs involve hallucinative drug use, death and, sacrifical slaughter ("1008 animals beheaded, the executioners ankle-deep"), and imagery surrounding blue flowers ("hyacinthus amethystinus") and blooming ("[e]xtravagant parts, their sex parts, blooming from their drugs"). This thematic and symbolical blend invokes ethnic fertility myths and drug-infused, ritualistic practices causing trancelike states of mind. The text's references to blue flowers inspire Western

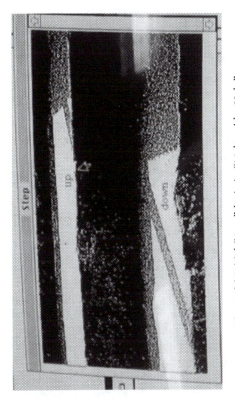

Figure 16 Initial "Step" lexia in "Mahasukha Halo"

Romantic imagery, supporting the metaphysicality of the poem. The overall effect of the sexual and often fecal language featuring in the work is an opaque turmoil of erotic titillation and corporeal abjection, which implants in the reader's mind the "[i]ndescribable misery" ("Azuria") of the otherworldly culture conveyed by the text.

Gess describes the genesis of his work as follows:

> It was a small and pleasant closure to an excursion begun six years previously, when I noticed the *Discover* magazine article about Bolter, Joyce, Moulthrop, Bernstein et al. on the same day I received a substantial grant from the Georgia Council for the Arts. I spent some of that money on my first computer (Mac Plus) and promptly proceeded to tinker with Storyspace – because, at the time, I felt that words were failing me . . ., and because I have always been attracted to art-making based in gadgetry (film cameras, electric guitars, hypertext). The thing I created was/is a whatsit, heavily influenced by a small Atlanta avant-garde sub-scene that savored loopy sexual tangents mashed into sci-fi, and by my own feeling that it was a much more interesting experience to get lost than to navigate. (Interview)

The "whatsit" Gess refers to can be understood as a genre-defying "oddity, an anomaly, something outside the usual categories" (Gess, interview). It was inspired by Carl Zimmer's (1989) *Discover* article, "Floppy Fiction," which presented hyperfiction as a pioneering and "elegant mechanism for escaping time-driven, one-way plots" (34). Similarly, MH "dispensed with narrative in favor of free association, clustering, circling," combined with un-signposted "background notes that readers might find themselves dropped into without being clearly informed that they were entering a sort of metadata demesne" (Gess, interview). The "small Atlanta avant-garde sub-scene that savored loopy sexual tangents mashed into sci-fi" refers to a group of local artists, writers, and musicians who were inspired by Burroughs novels like the Red Night trilogy, as well as New Narrative artists like Kathy Acker, Dennis Cooper, and filmmaker Warren Sonberg.

According to Gess, "these influences were less about sci-fi (for which consider William Gibson and Bruce Sterling) than sexual (especially transgressively sexual) overdrive" (interview).

Originally, Gess wrote MH as a supplement to *Perforations*, a local avant-arts / avant-theory magazine. Yet it found a more welcoming home at Eastgate, which embraced the work's defiance of genre, and whilst Gess could not convince Bernstein to publish it as a stand-alone work, the decision to release it in the *EQRH* "provided a graceful resolution and gesture of respect to an artist operating in deliberate opposition – disrespect! – to many of the highest principles of the new genre" (interview).

3.1.6 "Seasoned Heart" and "Love's Deserts": Robert Kendall's "A Life Set for Two"

Robert Kendall's "long narrative poem," "A Life Set for Two" (ALST), is one of the best-documented and researched works in the *EQRH* (e.g., Glazier 2001; Funkhouser 2007; Grigar 2018). A traversal by John Barber at the ELL was published on Vimeo (Grigar 2018d), and Grigar et al. (2018) dedicate a full chapter of *Rebooting Electronic Literature Vol. 1* to its documentation and preservation. The work was published in issue 2:4 of the *EQRH*, alongside Richard Smyth's *Genetis* (3.2.7), yet features 1996 as its year of publication. The work is unique in Eastgate's catalogue (Grigar 2018a) as Kendall created the language and graphics in Microsoft's Visual BASIC, and in that much of it consists of animated, noninteractive poetry, reserving its hypertextuality mostly to navigational elements. In alignment with the bookish roots of digi-modernist publishing, parts of the work featured "in a CD-ROM issue of *The Little Magazine*" and in the print magazine *Lips*, and the work itself emerged from a "multimedia PC installation" supported by the Pennsylvania Council of the Arts/ Interdisciplinary Arts Program ("Acknowledgments").

"A Life Set for Two" is one of the earliest digital-born poems showing animated or "kinetic" hypertext – a feature deployed by Kendall to engage readers in the "dynamic processes of thought and memory." Each individual screen shows kinetic poems between which readers can navigate by clicking the Onward button at the bottom or top of the screen (see Figure 17). Another novelty exhibited by the poem is the saturated

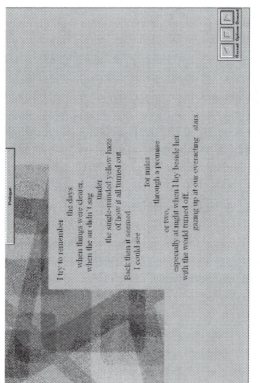

Figure 17 Screenshot of Robert Kendall's "A Life Set for Two"

multicolor scheme used for backgrounds, graphics, and fonts, as well as a variety of font types.

The poem revolves around an unnamed couple sitting in a café, symbolically enacting a situation "where the appetites of unresolved feelings feed on the past" ("How to Read This Poem"). The speaker recalls a fraught yet intense relationship of the past ("There once / was / a life set for two / here / somewhere"), which was tainted with miscommunication, disloyalty, dishonesty, suspicion, and jealousy. A figurative food menu offers free movement between different parts of the poem, which has "no prescribed linear order in which to read them" (ibid.). When the reader is ready to leave, they click on a button marked "The Check, Please," which will trigger a short, kinetic epilogue ("Then she was gone … ") before the software closes, allowing the reader to choose between "The End" (exit screen) and "The Beginning" (cycling back to the title screen).

The poem starts with a Prologue (black text on turquoise background, with an abstract graphic displaying intersecting and overlapping boxes) introducing a speaker trying "to remember / the days / when things were clearer" in their relationship with "her" before they started feeling submerged by the "single-minded yellow haze / of how it all turned out." In the last line of the first animated lexia, the words "overarching" and "overacting" continually replace one another as attributes of "stars," thus marking the transformation from the couple's mutual love to selfishness and obstinacy. Individual words replacing one another in one line of a stanzaic lexia recur throughout the work, starting in the title lexia's ever-morphing subtitle (e.g., "An Organic Lexiconjuring"; "A Virtual Telling"; "A Kinetic Text"). The Prologue is followed by a yellow box ("Past, past, who's got the past? Is it … ") (Figure 18) offering five different choices or "boxes" that readers can lift to find what's "underneath": "Under my hat?" "Under an obligation to pass away?" "Underhanded when underfoot?" "Under the name of ETERNITY?" and "Understood that it can go its own way?" All links except for the latter trigger an overlaid text box functioning as a dead end. However, choosing "Understood that it can go its own way?" textually concedes to the necessity to revisit the speaker's past rather than to deny or suppress it ("Yes. Let's follow it and see where it leads").

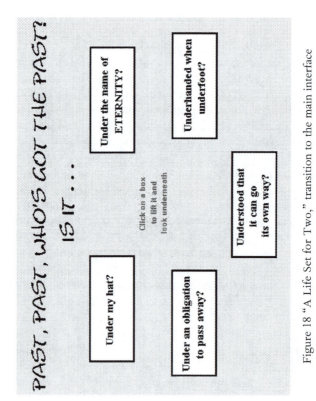

Figure 18 "A Life Set for Two," transition to the main interface

The work's main interface shows two different menus – one for the narrator and one for their lover. The menus display various symbolical "Café Passé" meal choices for "What Fed Me" (e.g., "Seasoned Heart," "Seefood," and "Manna from the Stars") versus "What Fed her" (e.g., "Dainties under Glass," "Naughty Treats," and "Love's Deserts"). The navigation box in the bottom right corner of the main interface allows readers to go "Onward," "Reread," and explore the text's "Options." They can toggle between kinetic and static text and adjust the kinetic text speed, the pause between lines, the interface configuration (e.g., how to display the Aftertaste control), and they can (de)activate Auto Continue. The same dialog window also shows the amount of text already "consumed." From the Options readers can leave the work entirely via the figurative "Exit to Present" button, or go back to the Opening Screen.

The work's bespoke visual design presents a stark contrast to the generic Storyspace environment that most works in the *EQRH* were published in. A small drop-down box in the top left corner allows readers to select between different "Added Seasoning[s]" such as the jealousy evoked by the "Touch of Another Man" and "Family to Taste." Another interactive box in the top right-hand corner gives choices between different "Aftertaste[s]" or background colors (blue, red, and black). Of further note is the "The Meat of Our Bodies" pathway from the "Café Passé" menu, which triggers a schematic representation of the lover's body, with text boxes representing her "Breasts," "Lips," and "Thighs," much like the sections of an animal's body, displayed for the butcher's eye ("Select a Cut"). With each "cut" the reader chooses, they remove that section from the display box as if they had physically consumed it.

In her extensive reading of ALST Grigar (2018d) remarks that Kendall's intent was to "creat[e] a new type of formal poetry that was born digital in response to" Oulipian works such as those by Raymond Queneau. These formal innovations marked a turn to interface poetics, which render the interface "an integral part of the interactive reading experience" (Kendall, personal correspondence with Mark Bernstein and Diane Greco, 2015). In ALST this idea is represented through strong color symbolism, the poetic manipulation of otherwise purely functional navigation and menu items, and "kinepoetic" animation (Grigar 2018d). In fact, ALST is primarily a work of kinetic, visual poetry and it only received the label "hypertext" to afford publication by Eastgate (Kendall, quoted in Grigar 2018d). It can thus be concluded that the *EQRH* transgressed hypertext even before the latter had become fully established as a medium and platform for creative writing, and many works that were not strictly speaking hypertexts were nonetheless referred to as such for lack of adequate terminology.

3.2 Short Fiction

In this section I move from the more poetically oriented works in the *EQRH* to the more narrative ones, also referred to as hypertext short fiction. As my analyses will convey, the works are as experimental and genre-bending in character as the poems and often cross the lines between fiction, poetry, and fine art.

3.2.1 "Longing for Morning": Mary-Kim Arnold's "Lust"

Hailed as a "miniature gem" (Coover 1993), Mary-Kim Arnold's poetic short fiction "Lust" is one of the best researched and critically most acclaimed Eastgate hypertexts (Grigar et al. 2018; see Figure 4). A traversal of it by Nicholas Schiller, read on a Macintosh SE, is available from the ELL at WSUV (Grigar and Schiller 2018). Comprising 38 writing spaces and 141 links, "Lust" uses Storyspace's text-only interface, arranged in short, often single-line paragraphs that resemble poetic stanzas.

The work takes the reader on a recombinatory journey of love, sex, desire, parenthood, and abuse. The weight and affective intensity of each concept varies, depending on the reader's interpretation and trajectory through the text. The text starts *in medias res*, without a title or front matter. A thematic prologue sets the scene of the narrative and introduces some of its key words and characters:

> Nearly naked
> this summer night
> sweet and heavy,
> he comes to her.
>
> This night, she follows him,
> sweat between them.

They speak of the child
and the summer sun
with words that yield
to the touch.

Core phrases like "Nearly naked," "he comes to her," "this night," "she follows him," and "the child" recur throughout the poem (Grigar 2018b), framing it as a story of "[s]exual lust, blood lust, lust for love" (ibid.), told from the homodiegetic perspective of her, and being embedded in a continually revolving day-and-night cycle. Whether or not "the child" is an actual, deceased, imagined, loved, desired, lost, and/or feared product of their love is left open to the reader's interpretation. So is the possibility of the relationship being a violent, abusive, or even murderous one ("She runs the blade along the surface of her skin . . . There is blood."), although the repetitive imagery ("She picks up the knife," "His carpet is stained with blood") strongly suggests physical as well as emotional abuse and the desire to kill for revenge.

Further into the work, the reader learns that the pronoun "he" could have four different referents, "or perhaps all of them" (Higgason 2004: 29): Jeffrey, Dave, John, and/or Michael. Each man has a dedicated, introductory node, parts of which recur throughout the text. This effect blurs the image of whom the narrator is talking about at any given moment, who the father of "the child" might be, and who the woman's rage is targeted at. Higgason (2004) uses this observation to underscore his reading of the work as a detective mystery. The female referent, conversely, is not framed as ambiguous. Nor is her name mentioned anywhere in the text. Although this does not necessarily mean that "she" is a single person, the unspecified personal pronoun generates textual cohesion, linking the narrative together around "her" as the focus and perceiving agent of the narrative.

In her interview Arnold explained that she had "minimal" involvement with the *EQRH*, other than publishing "Lust" in it. At the time she was an undergraduate student of Robert Coover's. She recalls submitting the manuscript of "Lust"

> for a class exercise, and at some point soon after, Bob said
> something to the effect of "we should have this published,"
> and then I think I met Mark, and I think I got a contract and
> then the work was out on floppy (!) disk.

Overall, Arnold's experience of working with Eastgate was a very positive
and rewarding one, which is echoed in a quote published on the folio blurb
of issue 1:2: "This experience [of writing and publishing 'Lust'] has been
a tremendous one for me, personally, academically, psychologically,
maybe even sexually." She describes the Storyspace medium as "the
most fertile, flexible, giving, nurturing place [she had] ever found to
write in, to be in, to share in," a stance echoed by many women and
feminist writers who turned to the digital medium as writing platform at
the time (Sullivan 1999).

3.2.2 "That's All She Wrote": J. Yellowlees Douglas's "I Have Said Nothing"

Like Arnold's "Lust," which co-appeared in issue 1:2, J. Yellowlees
Douglas's hypertext short fiction "I Have Said Nothing" (IHSN; version
1.0 of three in total, see Grigar 2018c) remains one of the best-known and
most thoroughly researched works in the *EQRH*. While it appeared in
the second issue, it was "the first one published" (1993), possibly due to
delays in *Intergrams*'s production. It is one of the few hypertexts to have
ever been reproduced in a print anthology (Norton 1997). A traversal of the
work, read by Philippe Brand, was recorded by the ELL at WSUV in 2017
and published in the first volume of *Rebooting Electronic Literature* (Grigar
et al. 2018). "I Have Said Nothing" was written on a Mac Portable and first
published on a 3.5-inch floppy disk. It contains 96 lexias and 205 links.

The key theme of the text is a sense of nothingness that has befallen the
female narrator in the light of two fatal, alcohol-induced car crashes, which
killed two of her brother Luke's girlfriends, Sherry and Juliet. The narrator
is dumbfounded by Luke's callous tendency to simply "replac[e] one body
with another." This is reflected in the titular nod to a freely translated
aphorism by St. Augustine: "I have done nothing but wish to speak; if
I have spoken, I have not said what I wished to say" [But I've said nothing].

Conceptually and formally, the text projects parallels between psychological and textual fragmentation, a technique explored by numerous hypertext writers in particular in relation to car crashes (see 3.2.6; Moulthrop 1994). Douglas combines the psycho-pathological theme with a general criticism of contemporary society, emphasizing drink- and drug-addicted youth culture and the simulacrum of Hollywood in American pop culture (Ensslin 2007).

Unable to fully vocalize her feelings, the narrator relates her memories in a fragmented manner. The work is structured like an inverted pyramid, bottle-necking all storylines accessed via default navigation in the programmatic cul-de-sac sentence "That's all she wrote" [The End]. The shift to third person evokes a frame narrative of an outside narrator (perhaps a psychologist) looking on and providing commentary on the intradiegetic narrator. This reflects Douglas's academic background in English literature, psycholinguistics, and medicine, particularly her interest in "the power of cognitive mapping for understanding intentionality and closure and an experiential completeness or incompleteness to the act of reading [as well as] the relationship between cognitive mapping, content and structure, . . . narrative and closure" (interview).

According to Douglas (interview), IHSN was originally intended for Mary Milton's planned interactive magazine *Gertrude*, which never launched. The piece had previously been rejected by another, more mainstream-oriented online magazine, which had recruited writers like Gerald Posner and Robert Coover, for being too dark. Douglas suspects "somebody might have mentioned [the unpublished work] to Mark [Bernstein]," upon which he "asked for it and offered to publish it, and I really didn't care in what form it got published." For Douglas, the main goal was to experiment with mapping cognitive complexities such as psychological trauma via tunnels, guard fields, Boolean operators and other system-specific functionalities.

3.2.3 "Obsessive Fragmentation": Kathryn Cramer's "In Small & Large Pieces"

Published in issue 1:3 (1994), Kathryn Cramer's short poetic hypertext fiction "In Small & Large Pieces" (ISLP) came bundled with Kathy

Mac's "Unnatural Habitats," first as two 3.5-inch floppy disks for Macintosh and PC, and later on a single CD-ROM requiring 2 MB RAM and a hard disk drive. The work was originally "produced with Storyspace 1.08 and used 875 K" (Grigar et al. 2019). A "dark fantasy" and "postmodern *Through the Looking Glass*" (folio back cover), Cramer's work aligns with numerous remediations of *Alice in Wonderland* in contemporary history of art, narrative, and digital culture (Salter 2015). The titular broken looking glass becomes a metaphor of "obsessive fragmentation" (blurb) throughout the text, and of how readers move between different types of texts, such as poems, handwritten notes, and captioned images "illuminates this moment of shattered self" (ibid).

"In Small & Large Pieces" consists of two main, interlacing parts: a narrative section that breaks into six chapters and can be read consecutively, by pressing the return key, and a poetry collection titled "The Mona Lisa Has Been Raped: Collected Poems." The chapters in the narrative part are titled "Chapter 1: The Effect of Living Backwards," "Chapter 2: Injury & Breakage," "Chapter 3: Anna, Phantomwise," "Chapter 4: The Unified Parent," Chapter 5: Scrambled Eggs," and "Chapter 6: The Mirror Shattered." As suggested by the title page (Figure 9), readers are encouraged to "hit return to continue," which will take them to the prefatory material and then on to the six chapters sequentially. The humorously named "poetry basement," then, alludes to the basement in the story, where mysterious, "awful" events happen. This architectural concept is reconfirmed by the location of the link to the section, in the lower half of the lexia, and somewhat set apart from the rest of the text in font size and style (Figure 19).

The poetry collection comprises thirteen short, lyrical poems, individual verses of which are interspersed into the narrative part. Cramer wrote the poems in her late teens and revisited them fifteen years later in the larger framework of her PhD project while studying German literature at Columbia University:

> I wrote . . . a lot of poetry as a teenager. And I would write and write . . . and then I decided it was not very good. And

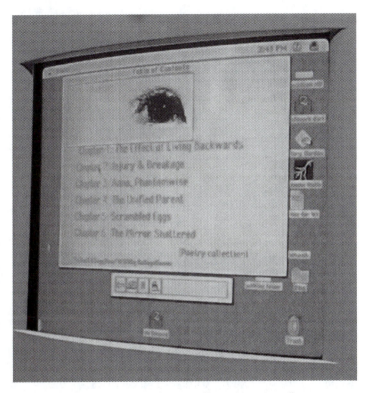

Figure 19 Contents page of "In Small & Large Pieces," courtesy of Grigar et al. (2019)

I would burn it, and I would start over. [The poems in ISLP] are the ones that survived the experience. . . . So I decided that since the character was . . . the age I had been, I could use as characterization the poems I actually wrote in that age range. (Cramer, interview)

Cramer emphasizes the importance of reading the work with a sense of humorous distance arising from this authorial age gap. Furthermore, she highlights the importance of associative, "synapse like" linkage in her hypertext.

"In Small & Large Pieces's" title page (Figure 20) shows a girl in Victorian clothing kneeling in front of a mirror. The way the mirror is designed and repeated in a similar, tombstone-like shape to the left of the figure suggests a graveyard setting. This gothic feel is reinforced by the wafts of mist running across the sky in the background, the praying gesture of the girl, and some barely legible snippets of palimpsestic, handwritten text, reading "by the sight of more blood." The text is thus framed as a horror remediation of Lewis Carroll's original *Through the Looking Glass*, a reflection of Cramer's background as an editor of horror fiction at the time.

Immediately following the title page is an epigraph taken from E.M. Forster's *Aspects of the Novel* (1927). It programmatically introduces the work's major structuring principle, which is the disruption of "sequence in chronology" and repeats in large fonts in the lexia, "That was the effect of living backwards." This reversion might reflect the materiality of reading via the return key, which paradoxically leads onward in the narrative whilst suggesting a reverse trajectory. As mentioned by Forster, reversing the order of events in a narrative cannot be done "without abolishing the sequence between the sentences," which again "is not effective unless the order of the words in the sentences is also abolished." Clicking on "the order of words" takes the reader to a lexia that displays a paragraph of text in exact reverse order. The Forster quote is illustrated by a linked poem displaying the alphabet in reverse order. The next click leads to a purely graphic lexia showing a human eye and nose on the left, a butterfly at the centre, and an open door on the right (Figure 21). Each element in the image is linked to a different onward lexia, some of which are graphic, others of which are textual – either handwritten or printed. Opening each lexia in turn results in the cognitive construction of a fragmentary frame of reference for the reader, with individual lexias suggesting themes like a potentially pedophile sexual relationship, an escape from home, drug consumption, images of stitching and quilting, as well as injury and blood.

Figure 20 Title page of "In Small & Large Pieces," courtesy of the Electronic Literature Lab

Figure 21 "In Small & Large Pieces" Butterfly lexia [Control pressed for links]

The default path proceeds from the butterfly imagery straight to the chapter overview of the narrative part. The unfolding story, told by a consistent heterodiegetic narrative, reads immersively and coherently. It introduces the protagonist Anna Miller, her twin sister, Annabelle, her brother, Martin, their parents, Norma and Martin, and Karl, "a man her father worked with" and presumably had a pedophilic love relationship with Anna. The first and sixth chapter jointly frame an embedded memory of parental neglect, drug abuse, suicidality, and a potentially drug-induced fantasy of Anna's. The frame narrative centers on a broken mirror, smashed in what turns out to be one of many fights between Anna and her "opponent" brother Martin.

The idea of breaking and sewing together is programmatic throughout ISLP, and in centering broken and mended body parts, Cramer foreshadows Shelley Jackson's canonical hypertext novel, *Patchwork Girl, Or A Modern Monster*, which appeared in 1995. The Frankensteinian motif materializes in a series of grotesquely rendered family crises that cause the parents' bodies to break apart whenever they are facing a crisis and that lead to Martin severing one of Annabelle's toes with a pair of pruning shears. In all instances, Anna becomes the mending force, taking care of sewing body parts back together and developing semantic-surgical strategies that end up reuniting her ruptured parents into a "parental unit" of complementary identity that ends up "skuttl[ing] spider-like into the kitchen and made itself cups of tea" [You will.] This surrealism is backed up with actual quotes from *Through the Looking Glass*, which Anna reads to her sister after the unified parent has closed the door behind themself.

"In Small & Large Pieces" was inspired by events that happened in Cramer's own family when she was a teenager:

> My brother and I used to really fight physically a lot. And so . . . climbing out the bathroom window and then coming around to attack from behind when my brother's trying to get [in bed], that happened, . . . there was an actual net mirror broken. And . . . I'm pretty sure I'm the person who threw the encyclopedia. . . . The title actually comes from a different broken mirror, . . . which was in a basement.

> And I think probably what happened in this case is like the
> hook it was on came loose, and it fell down on its own. . . .
> And I remember being very struck about the inversion of "it
> should be large and small pieces." And so the title comes
> from that and [a] clear memory of being both the person
> who had thrown the book and also jumping up to avoid.
> (Interview)

Cramer was already an established science fiction and horror writer when
she began to work and write for Eastgate in 1993. In fact, she had another,
novel-length hypertext work under contract with Eastgate with the working
title *Subpoena Vacation*. The work was an attempt "to ramp up the production values. And that just kind of never happened, because the kind of
fluidity in terms of composition that I had in *In Small & Large Pieces* was not
really possible with higher production values at that point" (ibid.). Thus
ISLP became the new standard for scoping works for the *EQRH*, confirm-
ing the relative success of "Lust" and "I Have Said Nothing" and providing
a reading experience that seemed feasible and value-for-money, for its
brevity, its intertextualization of genre fiction, and its pastiche technique.

Like other *EQRH* writers, Cramer used a more varied color palette (red,
blue, and grey) than was common at the time: "The screens I was working
with initially didn't even have gray pixels. They were black pixels, or they
were white pixels. . . . And we just got to the point where . . . we could have
color" (Interview). Cramer also laments the neglect with which the fonts of
her writing tend to be perceived, especially when reading from Windows
machines and emulators. "The type design was very specific and definite.
Like if a Macintosh has that in there, it's like my canonical type design," and
a lot of it gets lost when read on a PC.

Similarly, Cramer composed the cover art of the *EQRH* 1:3 (Figure 3)
showing a black-and-white grid pattern on a black background, with
contrasting white-and-black hands and one red, presumably bloody hand,
to reflect the content of Cramer's work. The writing on the cover is kept in
the same tricolor scheme, thus replicating the novelty of expanding the
standard black-and-white user interface. Cramer's fascination with patterns
and patching comes from a lifelong interest in collage and cut-up, which

also manifests in her recent work "Am I Free to Go" (tor.com), featuring "a lot of artistic similarities to *In Small & Large Pieces*" (interview).

3.2.4 "[I]t Doesn't Matter because It's Me": Judith Kerman's "Mothering"

Like most other writers gathered in the *EQRH*, American poet, performer, and artist Judith Kerman is best known for her print work, culminating in ten books or chapbooks of print poetry. Her *EQRH* short fiction "Mothering" remains her only foray into e-literature. Like Falco's *Sea Island*, "Mothering" is an attempt at remediating conceptually hypertextual print work into the Storyspace environment. To allow readers "an experience of the that which is not available in book format" [Acknowledgments], Kerman combined material from her 1978 prose poem "Mothering" and her 1978 verse play "Dream of Rain" into a multilinear array of female narrative voices. Her hypertext appeared with Larsen's "Century Cross" and Mantgem's "Completing the Circle" in 2:2, the only issue of *EQRH* containing three hypertexts. The work is scarcely documented, with no entry in key databases such as ELMCIP and the ELD, and only a short descriptive entry in French available on NT2 at the time of writing.

With 99 lexias and 1,607 links, "Mothering" capriciously weaves together themes and images that run through the text like "motifs," or "melodies" in "a piece of symphonic music" [Info]. The reader can choose which motif to follow or they can follow the 52 lexias of the default path, which correspond to the pages of the print version. Choosing lexias or motifs randomly will take the reader on threads representing specific characters, settings, or "mental process[es] such as dreaming" (Folio booklet, p. 20). These threads embed lexias that are not part of the default path, thus broadening the reader's understanding of specific narrative elements, such as spaces ("mountain"), objects ("knife"), and characters ("mothering"). According to Kerman, this makes her hypertextual *Mothering* "a better implementation [of her writerly intent] than the book" (ibid.), as it mediates the subconscious musings and anxieties of the third-person narrator in a more authentic way than the spatial linearity of print.

The narrator is a woman experiencing a form of postpartum depression. Feeling lonely and helpless, she muses upon and worries about various stages of maternity, from pregnancy to her child's adulthood, as well as earlier stages of her life and childhood. Her persona is introduced and textually represented in the initial lexia, [I], which marks part one of altogether four comprising the entire default pathway. Through an ever-shifting imaginative lens, the narrative voices shifts between different day-dreams, memories, anxieties, and projections of love, sex, birth, nursing, suffering, and loss, and her focus moves between a variety of male characters, including her father at his Jewish funeral, Alwin (potentially the father of the child), J. and R. (two further male friends), the Deep Sea Diver (her child, transfigured into a mystical sea creature and pedophilic lover), Plum (a childhood friend and possibly early lesbian love interest), and "the child." References to the latter, as well as to violent images like "the knife ... covered within blood" evoke strong affective parallels with Arnold's "Lust." That said, "Mothering" remains far more speculative, dissipated, and dreamlike in tone throughout.

Stylistically, the work projects the narrator's stream of consciousness. Short reflexive clauses and expressions are interspersed with typographical pause markers: periods surrounded by double spaces (" . "). This lends the piece a certain rhythmic quality, yet simultaneously communicates the speaker's breathless panic in imagining her helplessness and the "anger ballooning inside" [come it's all right] as she experiences a loss of control over her changing body. One of her internal voices, "mothering," represents a combination of her late mother's imagined voice and a more general superego that tries to talk sense into her ("mothering says, I can take care of both of you" [knife covered with blood]). Yet despite recurrent phases of confidence and relief (such as a rare, non-typographically disrupted lexia titled [the sound of birds]), she cannot help a strong sense of disconnect from her elusive maternal identity and the child, who "is listening to someone else."

In all, "Mothering" constructs motherhood as a condition to be simultaneously feared and desired and as a form of becoming that evolves over time and in continual fluctuations between self-loathing and self-love. The emphasis on subconscious forces at play in this process is evoked by the psychoanalytical allusions that permeate the text throughout, with references to "The Pleasure Principle" and the Law of the Father (Murray 1994). The narrator's phallogocentric anxieties culminate in dreams of penises (cf. 3.1.5), for example in the form of a "disembodied prick ... as big as she is, hanging their at eye level ... that follows her around like a puppy" [a visitation]. In Part III, the internal monologue finally settles on an imaginative letter to the narrator's friend J [Dear J], to whom she conveys that she has finally managed to "let go" of her shame and self-loathing: "it doesn't matter because it's me and that's all / there is." The text thus ends with a strong feminist statement and, subtextually, a call for (self-)compassion amongst women, whose role in society is fraught with judgment and the eternal struggle for acceptance.

3.2.5 Dodging the Storyspace Bug: Deena Larsen's "Century Cross"

American hypertext pioneer Deena Larsen features amongst the best-known e-literature artists represented in the *EQRH*. With 37 writing spaces and 359 links, her "Century Cross" (CC), is considerably shorter than the other two works in EQRH 2:2 with Kerman's "Mothering" (3.2.4) and Van Mantgem's "Completing the Circle" (3.2.6; "CC).

The only work in the *EQRH* that explicitly deals with Indigenous themes, CC includes two default paths that provide a highly coherent, bifurcating and later converging narrative. The Coyote pathway invokes the ancient Navajo myth of Coyote asking the prophetess Thought Woman for "a weapon more powerful than the weapons of the others" [Coyote 8] – arguably those of settler-colonists. Hinting that an even more powerful weapon will destroy everything, she attaches a "Nothing Pouch" on his nose, which he subsequently shows off to his friends. It turns out, however, that the Pouch's emptiness cannot convince them of its damaging potential and Coyote becomes the target of their ridicule.

In the Storyteller pathway, a first-person narrator, a government writer, spends the night at the federal building in Denver, Colorado, to complete unfinished work (Larsen claims this is autobiographical; interview). She begins to observe ghostly ongoings – picture frames crashing to the floor and invisible steps following her. In a frenzy, she bumps into Coyote from the other pathway, who still carries the Nothing Pouch around his nose. The metaleptic encounter leads to the narrator believing Coyote's story and deciding to tell stories about him whilst keeping the Nothing Pouch "closed tight" [Storyteller 12]. The crossover between storyworlds thus exposes the Storyteller narrative as a metafictional device, conveying a postcolonial plea to keep Indigenous stories and existences alive whilst exposing the destructiveness of colonialist tools of world domination via military force and data surveillance.

"Century Cross" was included in the *EQRH* to generate advance interest in Larsen's forthcoming work, *Samplers*, which consisted of eight other "vicious little hypertexts" (see Grigar et al. 2019). This work was the only *Samplers* story that could be used immediately without the further extensive reprogramming, so it was chosen (Larsen, interview). While like the other *Samplers*, CC includes a default reading path that could be triggered simply by pressing return, CC did not force a selection on the default path. Thus CC did not require using the bug in Version 1.25 where double linking the first space in a node would force a reader to choose between two or more default paths.

"Century Cross," like the other *Samplers*, emphasizes the intricacies of experimental-narrative linking, and on "how this form of storytelling is inherently connected to structure and infrastructure" (Slocum 2019). Larsen's structural concerns also led to other differences from early hypertexts, such as using underscores to mark hyperlinks (that would otherwise be invisible in the Storyspace interface) to direct the reader's attention to CC's complex story composition and layering. It also poses a semantically driven quandary: choose the default path or deviate from that "journey . . . to find other possibilities" [Directions] – of which there are too many to fully capture in this analysis.

Similar to Falco's poetic linking technique, Larsen embeds messages and passages in her line-by-line link labels in the Links overview available from the title page (Figure 22) in each *Sampler*. As the first page contains links to all other pages, this became a shadow narrative in each work. The CC story is a tongue-in-cheek rendition of some of the programming difficulties encountered when creating CC:

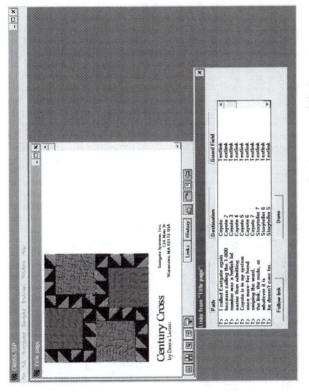

Figure 22 "Century Cross" title page with links

There Mark [Bernstein] never quite / believes me when
I swear / the work is haunted, and / I never press the
point. / Who would want to read / something so full / of
empty shadows, / of past demons anyway, / when you
know that / nothing you can do / will ever ease what /
has gone before? / Spending your time / wondering why
all / your ghosts come to you / or what rights the past /
has to keep its shades / busy coloring the now / is just
a waste of time. / Mark is probably / right to deny the /
right of existence to / such odd things as / ghosts. Or
pasts.

Figure 23 also shows Larsen's title image: a patchwork-style, right-pointing
swastika in cyan, magenta, and black: angles indicating the symbol's
original meaning of fortune and happiness, and the semantic shift marked
by its adoption by the Nazis. Larsen explains that the symbol functions as
a metonymy of the entire work:

The story is also about symbols and taking back symbols
and original meanings of lines and how we see the cross.
The center of rotation embeds the turning point and intersection in all of the stories in "Century Cross." (Interview)

She notes the possibility of looking at the linking structures between
individual lexias in the chart view. The color-coded paths correspond to
the cover image. A central Jane's Space in the middle of the cross can only
be reached by clicking in the chart view as there are no links in or out. The
significance of this feature is a combination of existentialist non-*dasein*, and
a nod to E Prime, a linguistic movement to rid English of any form of the
verb "to be," which is thematized in *Samplers*.

As a narrative innovation, Larsen introduces the convergence of default
paths into a metaleptic effect (cf. 3.1.3): to blend otherwise incompatible
storyworlds (the mythological Coyote with her own autobiographical alter
ego) to allow metafictional and philosophical reflection on the political and
specifically decolonizing powers of storytelling. On a more aesthetic,

Figure 23 "Completing the Circle's" "The Scotomic Episode" lexia, courtesy of Electronic Literature Lab

paratextual level, Larsen exploits pathway labelling as a new, platform-specific form of layering metafictional content onto a hypertext work itself – thus affording new ways of palimpsestic reading. Finally, the hidden Jane's Space revolving around ideas of non-being remediates a ludic device from videogame culture into e-literature: that of the Easter egg, which can only be found by accident or through specific interactive techniques to unlock additional features and meanings in a game.

3.2.6 A "Scotomic Episode": Michael van Mantgem's "Completing the Circle"

Like other works published in the *EQRH*, Michael van Mantgem's Storyspace hyperfiction "Completing the Circle" (CtC) has been largely ignored by existing scholarship (see Ensslin 2020a for its first ever scholarly analysis). Published with Larsen's CC (3.2.5) and Kerman's "Mothering" (3.2.4) in 2:2, the work comprises 216 writing spaces and 503 links.

"Completing the Circle's" titular allusion to medium-specific, circular rereadings and hypertext loops aligns serendipitously with the ongoing, iterative project of preserving e-literature exemplified by this book. Pre-web, experimental hypertext readers find themselves caught in a perennial pursuit for closure, thereby "completing the [hermeneutic] circle" not in the sense of actually closing the circle as a final product of reading, but rather in the sense of remaining caught in process of approximating completion, much like an unstoppable hamster wheel. In the narrative itself, the circular theme relates to the iterative mechanisms of life, love, desire, obsessive guilt, and traumatic reliving. These rotations can only be broken

> when events become completely clear, almost crystalline;
> when a choice, a single phrase, will create a very real future
> and an irretrievable past. That moment is so immediate that
> each choice becomes like a Venus Flytrap or The Yellow
> Brick Road. Keep in mind that there is only one direction
> and no possibility of return. Indeed choosing one path
> immediately and forever closes the other. (CiC)

These mutually foreclosing paths are resonant of the Aarsethian "paths not taken" (1997: 3), and reflective of Van Mantgem's attempt to combine determinist teleology and dynamic cyclicality both formally and conceptually. The text's paradoxical motto, that "a circle is always in the process of being completed and at the same time is always complete," presents readers with a "view from the protagonist [Haller]'s brain, a brain taken over by sex, delusions, mental collapse, and the desperate attempts to keep it all together." This "scotomic episode" (Figure 23), a medical term referring to partial obstruction or alteration in the field of vision, manifests in a combination of hypertext loops and more linear passages, which, however, criss-cross the protagonist's life in seemingly random, proleptically and analeptically organized memories. His condition is the result of an injury he inflicted on himself by deliberately crashing his car into the Mexican desert while escaping from his beloved yet estranged wife, Christina, with his much younger lover, Mary. A third female character, Carmen, appears in his musings at regular intervals, and whilst the impression arises that she is a prostitute he once had sex with, she also becomes the epitome of unachievable perfection in sexual and general life satisfaction.

"Completing the Circle" joins a canon of both print and hypertextual prose writings that deal with problematic masculinity, car crashes (Moulthrop 1993), and multiple personality phenomena (Ensslin and Bell 2012). A number of different narrative voices compete in CtC, including female characters, focalizing Haller from their critical point of view. This multivocality is augmented by the appearance of an intrusive narrator, who comments on Haller's condition as well as, metafictionally and metamedially, on the affordances of hypertextual writing for reader agency, but also its limitations for presenting complex mental conditions like Haller's. After all, hypertext leverages spatiotemporally linear human language and cannot live up to the challenge of authentically representing or simulating these conditions. To lift this dilemma onto a formal and metafictional level, occasional apostrophic reader addresses construct a metaleptic dialogue between the reader and the narrator. In these unidirectional dialogues, readers are engaged in a critical reflection on their own textual preferences and their perennial attempts at re-"playing the game of life" (CtC).

As the reading progresses, the textually implemented hermeneutic circle crystallizes into a frame narrative, which sees Haller being visited by Christina in hospital after the accident, and several embedded narratives that provide context for the car crash, including various episodes from Haller's earlier life with Christina, his affair with Mary, and sexual obsessions. However, since the protagonist is mentally unable to bring his life story into a coherent form, the narrator has to intervene to help readers construct a cohesive mental image of an incohesive state of mind. Each episode of the traumatic crash loop ends in a textually implemented dead end, which the reader can only escape by manually opening the link menu and choosing an exit option rather than simply hitting return or clicking on an available link in the lexia.

The genesis of CtC was in the early 1990s, when Van Mantgem was introduced to Storyspace while a student of Professor Brooks Landon's at the University of Iowa. Van Mantgem describes the encounter as "a moment on the cusp," which straightened the path to his later career as publishing manager at one of the world's foremost commercial gaming websites:

> This initial experience of working with hypertext greatly influenced my professional career. About the time my hypertext appeared in v2n2 [of the *EQRH*], I was working as an editor and author in the book trade. It was about this time too that the dotcom thing was happening, and I had the good fortune to make the jump. I landed with a startup called GameSpot (gamespot.com), which is now a property of CBS Interactive. . . . In essence, I guided the process of creating hypertexts for a mass market. By design none pushed the boundaries of interactive storytelling, but they did adhere to the basic principles of hypertext narrative as I understood them.

Thus, unlike most of his Eastgate peers, Van Mantgem transformed his experimental hypertext ideas into a career in commercial digital narrative, creating and publishing about "hypertexts for a mass market" and abdicating artistic iconoclasm for a financially more viable option.

3.2.7 "The Path of Madness": Richard Smyth's "Genetis: A Rhizography"

I have chosen to place my discussion of Richard Smyth's short "mystory" (Ulmer 2003) "Genetis: A Rhizography" (GAR) at the end of the fiction chapter in this book, in parallel to Kendall's *A Life Set for Two*, which closes the poetry chapter. Both works were published in the final issue of *EQRH* (2:4), and both stretch the limits of their genre to a medium-specific extreme – in Storyspace and Visual Basic respectively.

Structurally and intertextually, GAR is a creative response to *A Thousand Plateaus: Capitalism and Schizophrenia* (Deleuze and Guattari 1987) and numerous other theoretical works in literary psychoanalysis and technotextual epistemology, which Smyth had been studying during his graduate studies in English at the University of Florida. His dissertation on the rhetoric of hypertext composition, supervised by Gregory Ulmer, is "derived from the Renaissance Art of Memory as well as the poststructural concept of the rhizome" (Smyth 1994). Published only a year before GAR appeared as a creative-literary instantiation of Smyth's theoretical frame of reference, this "became the model for a new genre I proposed and theorized in my dissertation, the 'rhizography'" (interview).

Smyth's rhizographic writing integrates art and design (made by Roy Parkhurst) as well as audio ("violadagambaimprovisations" by Webster Early Williams Jr.) in the main text. In true hypertextual manner, it also interweaves a variety of existing genres, such as allegory, myth, and scholarly writing, into a densely cross-referenced, intertextual layer cake comprising 261 writing spaces and 344 links, that can only become comprehensible when read in mutual exegesis. Smyth performed a traversal of the work in June 2021 (Grigar et al. 2021b), thus filling a precarious gap in existing hypertext scholarship.

"Genetis: A Rhizography" can be read in "linear progressions that are similar to book reading" [INSTRUCTIONS], occasionally interspersed with with "bifurcations in the path, which will allow for a choice to be made" (ibid.). These forks are marked with bold letters in the first word of a lexia, or "cell" (a term chosen deliberately by Smyth to emphasize the work's interdisciplinary embeddedness in biochemical and anatomical concepts). The default path will be triggered by clicking on any word in a cell, or via the default return key. The deviating paths are called "memorypaths" and take the reader "on a spiraling course through the text." Thus the work blends the rational conventions of linear scholarly reading with those of deconstruction and associative musing, which were what hypertext represented to writers interested in representing cognitive processes and psychopathologies.

"Genetis: A Rhizography" blends hypertext storytelling with direct and indirect references to contemporaneous theories of the cyborg, of Lacanian psychoanalysis, of madness in literature, of the Florida School and its techno-epistemological take on poststructuralism, and affect as fully embodied, phenomenological account of reading and writing hypertext. The contents lexia [PLATEAUS] invokes "the five plateaus" or genres combined in Smyth's rhizography: "myth," "parable," "allegory," "legend," and "theory." These pathways are written in the characteristic style of each genre yet receive a medium-specific refashioning in each case.

"Myth" introduces an alternative, cyberfeminist creation myth, adapted from biblical Scripture and written in uppercase letters: "IN THE BEGINNING THERE WAS BIG DADDY AND BIG DADDY WAS A HAS-BEENING WHO WANTED TO WILL-HAVE-BEEN." It features the eight-breasted goddess "MOMMY," who turns out to have created Big Daddy in the first place in her "INFORMATRIX." This counter-genesis debunks the cyborg myth as an unrealistic dream, thus embedding a sharp critique of cyberfeminism's key metaphor.

Both "Parable" and "Allegory" are psychoanalytical tales of becoming and selfhood that reflect the author's troubled youth and personal experience of abuse, mental illness, and psychotherapy. "Parable" tells the story of "The Man in the Glass House," who cannot disconnect himself from his mother, Lacanian style, thus never succeeding in overcoming the mirror stage and finding his true self. He ends up committing suicide "with a big phallic gun / To prove his manhood" [b]. "Allegory" is an oedipal tale about a boy "with big hands [who was] born to a mommy who had eight breasts" [allegory 1]. He is addicted to his mother's milk, which adopts a similar intrusive, self-impeding role as the glass in "Parable" and prevents him from detaching his ego from his mother's body. He thus meets his downfall in a similar yet metaphorically alternative way to the man in "Parable."

"Legend" and "Theory," then, are explanatory sections that contextualize the three narrative paths. "The Legend of the Florida School" offers an account of the most influential voices and concepts informing Smyth's work: those of cybernetics and genetics, as well as "the advent of chaos theory, fractal geometry, and nonlinear dynamics – disciplines enabled by the computer – [which] fostered the emergence of hypertext" [CHAOS]. He mentions Milorad Pavic, Julio Cortazar, Jacques Derrida, and Italo Calvino as protohypertextual inspirations, and the tenets of poststructuralism, and especially the Florida School, as a key theoretical influence. His particular emphasis on dreams and other irrational, subconscious and cognitive phenomena as metaphors of hypertext writing comes to the fore in "Theory," where Smyth centers his discourse particularly on "The [phallic] Desire of the Mother" (Lacan 1994) and on madness in literature. The latter had just became a commonplace in literary scholarship, sparked by the work of Shoshana Feldman (1985), which Snyder had read in graduate school. The culmination of Smyth's authorial intent happens in [the path of madness], where he advises the reader that they "must be willing to experience madness" to fully appreciate his chosen format. "If this sounds too much for you, then go read a book" then becomes the author's key metafictional message to his readers. It can also be seen as the programmatic message that binds most if not all hypertexts in the *EQRH* together.

Smyth mentioned how painful he found it to have to include hyperlinked citations for each of the scholarly quotes he integrated in "Theory":

> I thought it would ruin the effect, the kind of "continuous dream" that John Gardner references in his book *The Art of Fiction*. Footnotes would pull the reader out of the experience I was trying to create ... I understood the legal concerns – and ultimately didn't really have a choice in the matter, if I wanted my work to be published – but this ultimately undermined the kind of radical ethos that hypertext, with all of its invocation of poststructural and

> postmodern tenets, promised: a kind of utopian deliverance
> from uptight literate values. (Interview)

Furthermore, being a tenure-track assistant professor of English at Hamline University (MN), Smyth felt it was an exciting prospect to be publishing his work in a journal that "would give me a broader, more academic audience, one that was more 'establishment' in terms of providing the kind of academic publication that could count toward tenure" (interview).

"Genetis: A Rhizography" broadened the experimental field of pre-web hypertext in a variety of ways. It offered a rare form of multimodality in text-oriented Storyspace during the "narrow window of time . . . before the web became so image-heavy" (interview). Roy Parkhurst's expressionist artwork (see Figure 24 for an example) amplifies the psychotic undertones of the literary text, and it foreshadows later developments in e-literature toward multimedia art and collaborative authorship. Smyth further revolutionized the use of genre by introducing a platform-specific mash-up of narrative forms, interweaving them with scholarly writing in pastiche form. However, unlike Giuliano Franco, who we will turn to in the following section, Smyth never moves to an actual scholarly-functional style of writing, thus keeping the entire rhizography expressive in tone and intent.

3.3 Nonfiction

Bernstein's willingness to experiment with new forms of medium-specific, nonlinear publishing extended to one meta-scientific, meta-scholarly work, *Quam Artem Exerceas? The Life and Times of Bernardino Ramazzini* (*QAE*), by Italian ergonomic physician Giuliano Franco. In an unprecedented and hitherto unparalleled effort, Franco deployed Storyspace to remediate and annotate an early eighteenth-century treatise in early occupational medicine (translated into English by Wilmer Cave Wright in 1940) via a hypertextual, biographical, and societal ecology of the original author's magnum opus. Published in issue 1:4, with a whopping 244 lexias and 562 links, *QAE* is a masterpiece in pre-web informational linking and structural transparency.

The Latin title means "What do you do for a living?" It refers to a question the subtitular early modern physician, Bernardino Ramazzini

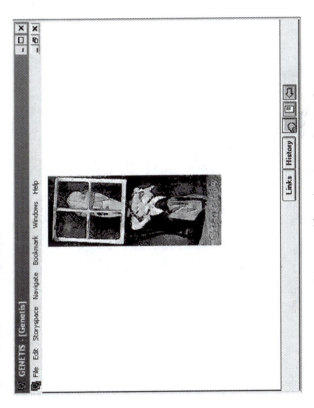

Figure 24 Roy Parkhurst's cover art in *Genetis*

(1633–1714), often asked his patients to identify work-related causes of diseases they presented with. Ramazzini, around whom Franco's essay revolves, is commonly known as the father of occupational medicine. Franco, who was a professor of occupational medicine at the Universities of Pavia and Modena at the time he authored the essay, dedicated much of his research to "advancing the use of hypertext learning tools" (1:4 folio booklet: 15), and a long list of his publications that informed his scholarly edition of *QAE* is integrated in the hypertext.

Quam Artem Exerceas? appeared along with Rob Swigart's "Directions" (see 3.1.3) in 1:4. Whilst both texts seek to represent aspects of scientific historiography (see Swigart's inclusion of a now historical version of the periodic table of elements), Franco's approach aims for maximum scholarly authenticity, clarity, and cohesion. He even included reproduced images from Ramazzini's work, such as the original title page (Figure 25) and graphic images (see Figure 3 for the folio's front cover, depicting an early modern chemist with a test tube).

Quam Artem Exerceas? is divided into clearly delineated sections, placing Ramazzini's groundbreaking treatise, "De morbis artificium diatriba" ("Diseases of Workers," 1700) within the historical, cultural, philosophical, medical, and economic context of its time, as well as accounting for some of Ramazzini's biographical circumstances that led to the creation of "De morbis." By clicking on bolded links in the text, readers can navigate the different contextual sections of the treatise with ease, thus learning more about Enlightenment thought, early industrial inventions, and early modern literature and art. At the core of *QAE* lie two large quasi-encyclopedic, meticulously laid out hypertext maps, or grids, both of which are adapted from "De morbis" and color-coded: the blue map (Figure 26) contains individual lexias dedicated to individual professions and their associated "human activities," such as "stone cutting," "soap production," and "printing."

The larger, red map explains common ailments that Ramazzini associated with specific types of occupational activities, including the mostly sedentary activities of tailors, shoemakers, nuns, and "literary men" – a term that denoted members of what is today commonly known as creative, knowledge-based workers (e.g., professors, lawyers, designers). The

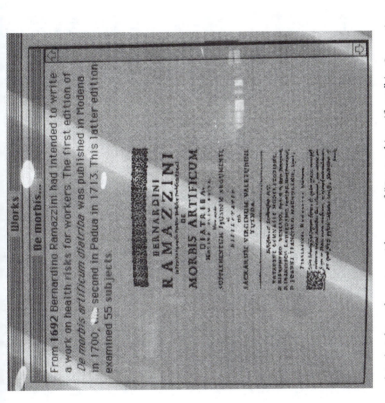

Figure 25 Reproduced eighteenth-century title page of "De morbis artificum" in *Quam Artem Exerceas?*

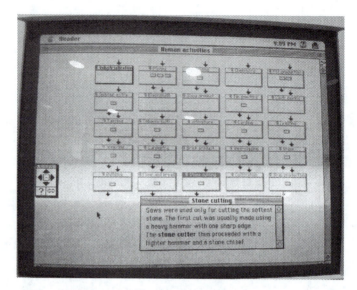

Figure 26 Blue map of "human activities," such as "stone cutting"

symbolically readable occupational risk map (with red connoting danger, as per conventional street signage) is intricately interlinked (Figure 27), thus depicting the complexity yet nonetheless scholarly transparency that characterizes Ramazzini's original essay.

Clearly, the WWW has over the years become the prime publishing platform for scholarly hypertext and bibliographic editions. Standards and protocols like TEI, XML, and Cambridge Core have been developed to digitize print materials and make them accessible and searchable widely. However, with hardly of these standards in common practice in the early 1990s, Franco's work manifests a key precursor to contemporary text editing, encoding, and archiving.

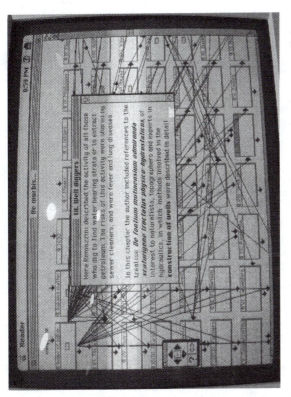

Figure 27 Red map of occupational risks with an exemplary lexia on well diggers

3.4 Print Paratexts

The print paratexts of the *EQRH* represent an early form of cross-platform research creation that requires individual scholarly treatment. Their material significance for pre-web hypertext is distinctive, and the specific combination of folio and data carrier was characteristic and idiosyncratic of Eastgate's publishing approach. Furthermore, the information given in the folios was critical to installing, navigating, and understanding the hypertexts published on the data carriers because no other crowdsourced or otherwise participatory online knowledge sharing was available at the time.

The booklets start with (often extensive) installation instructions for PC and Mac, followed by specifics on how to navigate, interact with, and/or "read" certain works. The last part of each issue contains introductory essays, acknowledgments, author bios, and commentaries (two to eleven pages long) by either the issue authors themselves, or an external expert (Moulthrop, in 1:2). Although in some issues they only constitute less than 10 percent of the entire booklet, or are completely missing (in 1:3 and 1:4), they merit particular attention because they form a scholarly-creative, transmedial bridge between the works and their copublished metadata. The editors' inconsistent approach to their inclusion and placement suggests that the *EQRH*'s publication format served as a hyper- and peritextual sandbox (Genette 1979). Peritexts are the functional paratexts immediately and physically surrounding a core text, such as jacket blurbs and contents pages in print. With Eastgate's and Mark Bernstein's strong editorial stamp on the shipped folios, the peritext in much pre-web e-literature was anything but missing or dysfunctional (cf. Tomaszek 2014). In fact, it was as seminal as the instruction booklets in commercially traded video games up until the 2010s, and indispensably complemented the hypertextual reading experience.

Together, the booklets contain eight commentaries. In 1:1 and 2:3, Rosenberg adds extensive details. "Openings: The Connection Direct. Personal Notes on Poetics" (1:1, pp. 5–16) conveys that his intent transcends and subverts the constraints of artistic communication. What matters instead is the "energy transaction layer" (5) between artist and "receiver," which circumvents the finiteness of understanding and leads to a "heightened state of attention" and to "new connections" being formed in the beholder. Rosenberg further highlights the spatial affordances of writing as a storage and space for movement. He proposes "direct access communication" (10) as the key goal of his diagrammatic word art, which operates via asyntactic juxtaposition and leaves "all slots open" so as to enable connectivity between all points in the pattern and allow "true openness for poetry" (12).

In the much shorter "Foldings, to the Chord Trellis Relate-Shape Draw: Notes for the appearance of *Diffractions through*: The thirst weep ransack (frailty) veer tide elegy and *The Barrier Frames:* Finality crystal shunt curl chant quickening giveaway stare" (2:3, pp. 19–22), Rosenberg reemphasizes the importance of "simultaneities" (19) in his cluster art and laments the reader's "all-consuming" "yearn for structure" (20). The main intent that comes across here is the challenge to put words "simply *there together*," thus foregoing any syntactic or semantic relationships. He uses metaphors from zoology ("metamorphosis") and musicology ("polyphony") to frame his work both as morphing bodies and simultaneous chords, which render the poem not as "a presentation of wisdom but a simple catalysis of the ambient reader-self, latent, ripe for the making of its own wonderful music" (21–22).

Perhaps the most idiosyncratic of all *EQRH* folio booklets is the one for 1:2. Following minimalistic installation and navigation instructions (less than a page) from Eastgate, Douglas prefaces the issue with her own sarcastic take on reading "I Have Said Nothing" ("The Quick and the Dirty"). She explains her motives as the "avoidance of pain" (2) that she might inflict on herself and the reader by choosing a new technology for a new type of narrative. Her intent is to maintain causality as "the root of all narratives" (2) and to use loops in a way that won't alienate the reader. She is mindful of the "dubious" nature of the freedom that comes with choice and places closure in the hands of the hypertext reader. Her metanarrative thus reveals key aspects of the primary text that may escape the novice reader and lends Douglas' work a sense of tongue-in-cheek vulnerability.

Moulthrop's equally humorous response to Douglas' preface, "The Crash of Nothing into Something" (5–13), is dedicated to the "logic of car crashes" (8) in pre-web hypertext fiction. Invoking Joyce's *afternoon: a story*, Monica Moran's hypertext comic *Ambulance* (published by Electronic Hollywood in 1993), John McDaid's *Uncle Buddy's Phantom Funhouse* (1992), and his own *Victory Garden* (1991), Moulthrop accounts for the Americanness of early hypertext fiction and its rootedness in Hollywood culture – a culture that mainstreams "panapocalyptic" (9) destruction, violence, fatality, and fragmentation, and embeds them in an ever repeating, naturalized loop of desensitizing predictability. This loop is reflected in the structural affordances of Storyspace in particular and thus becomes a metafictional metaphor for hypertext writing as a whole. For Moulthrop himself composing the essay "was a joyful labor that I still think of fondly. It got me writing semi-seriously about disruption aesthetics, and about the fact that hypertext had any kind of definable aesthetic at all" (interview). As with much of the work published by Eastgate at the time, the true significance of Douglas's and Moulthrop's exegeses for understanding pre-web hypertext writing as a media-historical and culture-specific epiphenomenon of the early days of the Web cannot be overstated. In many ways, both are programmatic for the entire first generation of hypertext and deserve to be lifted out of the hidden confines of the scholarly neglected *EQRH*.

Falco's short essay "Arriving at the Hypertext Poem" (2:1, pp. 21–22) sketches the poet's experimental program in close alignment with the other *EQRH* authors: to explore the nonlinear affordances of the medium with the goal to derationalize narrative. It particularly echoes Rosenberg's idea to circumvent the page's ordering function in the interest of greater collaboration between writer and reader. Every "segment of language (or stanza, if you prefer) is rooted in the core of the poem, which is a complex of emotions and ideas not easily translated into prose" (22). Individual spaces create a "wordscape [that] the reader is free to wander alone" – within the constraints of the effect evoked by the poems yet at their own interpretive discretion. In contrast to Rosenberg, then, Falco explicitly embraces the temporal constraints of reading as movement through space, yet his poetic intent is similarly centered around a certain type of transactional, affective energy that remains at the core of the reading process.

In "The Trickster, or, How I Learned to Love the Bomb" (2:2, pp. 15–16), Larsen echoes Douglas's insistence on creating a reading experience that is navigationally complex yet still anchored in core principles of cause and effect. For her, hypertext offers three-dimensional structures for writing and reading. *Samplers* in general and CC is an experiment in layered quilting "in a very formalized, closed system" (16) that explores the swastika in all its historical manifestations.

In her own scholarly preface to 2:2, "Literary Hypertext from a Writer's Point of View" (2:2, pp. 17–20), Kerman examines the implications of medium-specific narrativity in hypertext. She preempts Bolter and Grusin's later work on remediation as a process of refashioning and autonomization (1997) and (with a nod to Rosenberg) centers the tensions between linguistic linearity and interactivity as a core challenge of new media narrative. Critical of the allegedly participatory affordances of the medium, she demands instead that "to shape the experience, the author must limit choice" (19) rather than generate excessive freedom. An excess of choices, warns Kerman, runs a risk of obscuring the rhetorical intent and derailing the delicate "tension between expectation and outcome" inherent in the hyperlink.

Kendall's preface to 2:4, "Words and Mirrors: Confessions of an Electronic Poet" (pp. 15–21), forms the final author preface in the *EQRH*. In a similarly self-effacing programmatic tone as we have seen in other *EQRH* prefaces, the poet draws the reader's attention to the material affordances and performativity of hypertext. He imagines hypertext reading as an experiential, illusionist "little dance" that due to its "malleable" character can simulate "the squirming, restless contents of memory" (16–20). He is aware of hypertext's medial constraints that cannot fully "replicate thought and memory" (20), yet he invokes his readers' "trust in the pixels [and] the slippery virtual text" as they remove the fixity of the printed page whilst preserving "the integrity and direction of a book" (16). Kendall thus adds a key theoretical facet of early hypertext theory, which sees the reader as "part of the act" (17) on stage rather than a passive recipient.

Seen in their totality, then, the metafictional peritexts in the *EQRH* encapsulate many of the key tenets later elaborated by leading hypertext theorists like Landow, Hayles, Aarseth, Bolter, and Ryan. Key for our understanding of small-form literary hypertext, they are rooted in writers' experimental commitment to exploiting the pre-LED screen's "flickering signifiers" (Hayles 1993), to the emergent multimodality and non-fixity of verbal art, to the delinearization and derationalization of words and narrative, and to disrupting the normalized role of the reader as detached consumer.

4 Conclusion

The *Eastgate Quarterly Review of Hypertext* emerged at a historic threshold between print and online culture and reflects the uncertainties facing the looming age of late print and the early Web. It represents an editorial attempt to address the need for medium-conscious innovation at a time when publishing itself came to stand on increasingly shaky ground. The reasons for the *EQRH*'s sudden demise comprise a combination of complex variables: with the World Wide Web as only one of many potentially viable options for massified networked media, the future of hypertext as a form of textual organization and publishing platform was far from obvious. So was the future of poetry and fiction in a postmodern world that was on the verge of exhausting its own limitations and preparing for a return to plot and closure. A new form of publishing needed new audiences, and Eastgate's exploratory business model did not stand the test of time, given the dearth of hypertext material to be published and the scarce royalties to be gained from its sales. Nonlinear experimentalism was fast moving to open online platforms, and with the advent of Flash in the mid-1990s, many writers that could potentially have supplied Eastgate with new material were developing interests in less text-heavy, multimedia forms of online interactivity.

That Eastgate's commercial sales model was inappropriate for e-literature was borne out by the evanescence of *EQRH*'s follow-on platform, *Tekka*, which Bernstein launched to match the shift to more multimodal forms of electronic writing. *Tekka* still came with a hefty price tag, thus reiterating the clash between print capitalism and avant-garde writing. Other, open-access e-literature platforms that started in the 1990s, like Eastgate's *Hypertext Reading Room* and Falco's *The New River*, survived because they embraced the open-access Web for small-form literary publishing and overcame the barriers to access posed by physical data carriers. *The New River* also had the support of Virginia Tech University. In return, the move to straightforward online publishing meant sacrificing the opportunity for structurally deeper hypertextuality represented by Storyspace – a commitment Eastgate upholds to the present day.

However, the burgeoning communities surrounding hypertext and interactive fiction writing in Twine and Inform 7 have proven that hypertext writing can generate large international audiences of readers and writers, with branches into mass media culture like streaming television (see Netflix's *Bandersnatch*, for example). With the takeover of social media culture, then, the future of the *EQRH* "is already in place in technologies like wattpad, kindle, kobo, D2D, and Findaway Voices" (Mac, interview). And yet, almost two decades before the social media explosion, Eastgate's authors were already engaged in forming a proto-participatory community, encouraged and fostered by Bernstein and his team. Thanks to the preservation efforts made by the ELL and its traversal program, this community has retained or regained its cohesiveness in contemporary participatory culture.

The demise of the *EQRH* as a vignette of a fleeting yet critical historical moment should not be a reason to hide or dismiss its pioneering achievements and lasting legacy for the e-literature community in particular. Pre-web hypertext as represented in the *EQRH* summatively modeled numerous artistic techniques and theoretical concepts that were to become commonplace from the late 1990s onward. Firstly, its works demonstrated how medium-specific textuality can disrupt conventional notions of poetry and narrative through delinearization and cyclicality. Throughout the *EQRH*, the latter are represented in terms of intersecting paths (Mac), respatialized language and typography (Rosenberg, Falco, Kerman), mashup and pastiche (Gess, Swigart), ritualization, and mystification (Gess). Larsen, Swigart, and van Mantgem's works show that delinearization and interweaving can generate new, platform-conscious forms of interactional metalepsis (Ensslin and Bell 2021), whether this happens on a full, ontological level, with characters from different worlds meeting in the same space (CC), or on a purely rhetorical level, through exegetic and pictographic reader address (CtC and "Directions"). Other works engage with the implications of delinearization for the disruption of genre conventions ranging from myth to parable, from horror to science fiction, and from surrealist children's fiction to cyberfeminist pastiche.

A particular concern that permeates the *EQRH* relates to hypertext as an experimental cognitive mapping tool. The *EQRH*'s writers offer a range of artistic approaches to representing and experiencing complex cognitive processes relating to memory (Cramer, Kerman), dreams (Gess, Smyth), trauma or depression (Douglas, Van Mantgem). Furthermore, as Moulthrop's commentary in 1:2 demonstrates, the early hypertext community was acutely aware of its culture-specific frame of reference, which collectively formed a response to Hollywood simulacra. The predominance of car crashes in pre-web hypertext is metonymic of this awareness. The disruptive forces at work in the *EQRH* thus epitomize the "ambivalent relationship" of digital modernist writers to mass media and pop culture (Wollaeger and Dettmar 2014: ix), and they do so in a rare sampling of works that shared a social-material interest in the affordances of Storyspace and HyperCard in particular.

Being published in the *EQRH* was as strategic and career-forming for some as it was haphazard and coincidental for others. Whilst for some *EQRH* writers, like Van Mantgem and Kerman, their contributions remained their only forays into hypertext, others consider their contributions to be part of a longer, ongoing process of developing nonlinear, multimodal writing experiments. Rosenberg, for example, has been developing his interactive work in the form of spatial hypertexts ever since the late 1980s. At the time of my research he was adding sound to *Diagrams Series 7*, no. 3, which left him "grappling with how to properly introduce the linearization of sound into a totally nonlinear, spatial environment" (interview). In the early 1990s many in the hypertext community knew his work from conferences. Yet, arguably, Bernstein's intervention put his work on the radar of international hypertext scholarship more widely. Cramer's "In Small & Large Pieces" integrates poems she wrote in her youth, thus lending the work connectivity and continuity. At the same time, it has "obvious connections" with her later writing and art, such as the lexially structured "Am I Free to Go?" (Cramer 2012) and her visual collage work (Cramer 2020). Larsen's "Century Cross" was essentially a gap filler for another work that had "fallen through at the last minute" (Larsen, interview), and the choice fell upon it because it was the only one in *Samplers* that did not have the Storyspace bug. Larsen has been authoring and teaching hypertext ever since, and her web hypertexts *Disappearing Rain* (2000) and *Marble Springs 3.0* (2012) are read and taught in digital fiction classrooms around the world.

The lore of hypertext is as fragile and evanescent as it is important to nurture and record. This book has demonstrated how it can be used as a systematic, ethnographic method to reconstruct a watershed moment in recent publishing and media history. Combining lore with media and platform-conscious text analyses, this book amplifies our understanding of the roots of a fast-growing community of digital writers, artists, and scholars. It is an exercise in preservation and documentation, lifting forgotten and obsolescent material into the limelight and giving a voice to often neglected practitioners that were key to forging paths to digital art – verbal and otherwise – as we know it today.

Appendix
Technical Details of Individual *Eastgate Quarterly Review of Hypertext* Works

Title	Author	EQRH	Publication date[32]#(s)	Production platform[32]#(s)	Size[46]#/scope	Technical requirements
Intergrams	J. Rosenberg	1:1	1988, 1990, 1991, 1992, 1993	HyperCard	2.03Mb; 11 works	3.5-inch floppy for System Software 7.x; Mac OS 8.x/9.x; Hypercard 2.x or HyperCard Player
Lust	M.-K. Arnold	1:2	1994, 1998	Storyspace	28.7 k; 38 spaces; 141 links	3.5-inch floppy for System Software 6.x–9.x; later CD-ROM for Mac OS X v10 and Windows 98
I Have Said Nothing	J. Y. Douglas	1:2	1994, 1998	Storyspace; Mac Portable	76,4 k; 96 spaces; 205 links	3.5-inch floppy for System Software 6.x–9.x; later CD-ROM for Mac OS X v10 and Windows 98
In Small & Large Pieces	K. Cramer	1:3	1994	Storyspace	876 k; 513 spaces, 2625 links	3.5-inch floppy (x2) for Mac/PC, System Software 7.x and Mac OS 8.x/9.x; later CD-ROM: 2 MB RAM

Unnatural Habitats	K. Mac	1:3	1994	Storyspace; SuperPaint	1400 k; 96 spaces; 288 links	3.5-inch floppy (x2) for Mac/PC, System Software 7.x and Mac OS 8.x/9.x; later CD-ROM: 2 MB RAM
Quam Artem Exerceas?	G. Franco	1:4	1994	Storyspace	710 k; 244 spaces; 562 links	3.5-inch floppy; CD-ROM; System Software 7.x–9.x (floppy); Mac OS X v10.0–10.3
Directions	R. Swigart	1:4	1989–1994	HyperCard	1.7 MB; integrated work	3.5-inch floppy; CD-ROM; System Software 7.x; Mac OS 8.x, 9.x
Mahasukha Halo	R. Gess	2:1	1995	Storyspace	343.9 MB; 308 spaces; 759 links	3.5-inch floppy for System Software 6.x–7.x and Mac OS 8.x–9.x; CD-ROM for System Software 7.x; Mac OS 8.x–10.3.x; Windows 95
Sea Island	E. Falco	2:1	1995	Storyspace	0.08 k; 221 spaces; 1039 links	3.5-inch floppy for System Software 6.x–7.x and Mac OS 8.x–9.x; CD-ROM for System Software 7.x; Mac OS 8.x–10.3.x; Windows 95

(Cont.)

Title	Author	EQRH	Publication dateth32#(s)	Production platformth32#(s)	Sizeth46#/ scope	Technical requirements
Century Cross	D. Larsen	2:2	1995	Storyspace	138.9 k; 37 spaces; 359 links	3.5-inch floppy; CD-ROM for System Software 7. x; Mac OS 8.x–9.x
Mothering	J. Kerman	2:2	1995	Storyspace	300.7 k; 99 spaces; 1607 links	3.5-inch floppy; CD-ROM for System Software 7. x; Mac OS 8.x–9.x
Completing the Circle	M. van Mantgem	2:2	1995	Storyspace	628.9 k; 216 spaces; 503 links	3.5-inch floppy; CD-ROM for System Software 7. x; Mac OS 8.x–9.x
The Barrier Frames	J. Rosenberg	2:3	1996	HyperCard	198.1MB (incl. DT); 9 works	3.5-inch floppy; System Software 7.x; Mac OS 8.x–9.x
Diffractions Through	J. Rosenberg	2:3	1993, 1996	HyperCard	198.1MB (incl. TBF); 1 work	3.5-inch floppy; System Software 7.x; Mac OS 8.x–9.x
A Life Set for Two	R. Kendall	2:4	1996	Visual BASIC	0.4 k; integrated work	3.5-inch floppy for System Software 6.x–7.x; Mac OS 8.x–9.x; Windows

Genetis: A Rhizography	R. Smyth	2:4	1996	Storyspace	616.2 k; 261 spaces; 344 links	3.5-inch floppy for System Software 6.x-7.x; Mac OS 8.x-9.x; Windows 95/98; CD-ROM for Windows 95/98

Glossary

Aleatoric – based on chance rather than predetermination. In e-literature theory, aleatoric processes can be programmed into a work of verbal art to augment its playful, generative, or unpredictable effects in response to user input and interaction. In hypertexts, aleatoric link structures can, for example, lead to different mental images of plot, character, tone, or setting, and/or reduce readers' sense of control of textual navigation and comprehension.

Guard fields – Boolean expressions that change a reader's path according to lexias they have or haven't visited before. They can break loops or cycles in a Storyspace hypertext reading experience.

Emulation – digital process in which an original piece of software and/or hardware is executed on a platform for which it was not originally produced or intended. Typically yet not exclusively, emulators are used to recreate obsolete technological processes and environments.

Folio – in the context of Eastgate's hypertext publishing, folios are the vinyl and cardboard envelopes in which the works were published, shipped, and displayed – first on 3.5-inch floppy disk, and later on CD-ROM. Folios also contained paratextual meta-information in the form of printed booklets and advertisements.

HyperCard – default hypermedia application shipped with Macintosh computers for the HClassic Environment from 1987 to 2004. Conceptualized as a flat-file database with a graphical, user-modifiable interface and a built-in programming language (HyperTalk), HyperCard provided an unprecedented range of creative tools, including multimodal designs and interactivity that went well beyond hyperlinks.

Jane's Space – equivalent of video game easter eggs; in Storyspace, the term refers to writing spaces without inbound links. These spaces have to be found in unconventional ways, for example by entering a URL or search string, or by navigating through a map view; named after hypertext writer and critic Jane Yellowlees Douglas.

Lexia – digital, on-screen text space, also known as "*texte-à-voir*" (Bootz 2005). The term was originally coined by Roland Barthes in the more abstract sense of "unit of reading," and later developed as a key concept in hypertext theory by George P. Landow. A typical hypertext lexia contains one or more hyperlinks, which enable readers to choose different pathways for every reading, thus generating different mental images of the text, or indeed different textual manifestations.

Sneakernet – early, pre-Web, proto-social media network nurtured by the early Eastgate community, where physical copies of works were exchanged on data carriers during events like conferences, readings and seminars.

Storyspace – dedicated, proprietary hypertext authoring, editing, and reading tool developed by Jay David Bolter, John B. Smith, and Michael Joye in the 1980s and presented at the first international Hypertext conference in October 1987; available for Macintosh and Windows; distributed and maintained by Eastgate Systems. Its key functionalities include writing spaces, links, maps, and notes. Storyspace is currently at version 3.9.0.

References

Primary Works

From the *Eastgate Quarterly Review of Hypertext*; Watertown, MA: Eastgate Systems

- Arnold, Mary-Kim (1994) "Lust," 1:2.
- Cramer, Kathryn (1994) "In Small & Large Pieces," 1:3.
- Douglas, J. Yellowlees (1994) "I Have Said Nothing," 1:2.
- Falco, Edward (1995) *Sea Island*, 2:1.
- Franco, Giuliano (1994) "*Quam Artem Exerceas*?" 1:4.
- Gess, Richard (1995) "Mahasukha Halo," 2:1.
- Kendall, Robert (1996) "A Life Set for Two," 2:4.
- Kerman, Judith (1995) "Mothering," 2:2.
- Larsen, Deena (1995) "Century Cross," 2:2.
- Mac, Kathy (1994) "Unnatural Habitats," 1:3.
- Moulthrop, Stuart (1994) "The Crash of Nothing into Something," 1:2, pp. 5–13.
- Rosenberg, Jim (1994) "Intergrams," 1:1.
- Rosenberg, Jim (1995) "The Barrier Frames" and "Diffractions Through," 2:3.
- Smyth, Richard (1995) "Genetis: A Rhizography," 2:4.
- Swigart, Rob (1994) "Directions," 1:4.
- Van Mantgem, Michael (1995) "Completing the Circle," 2:2.

Carpenter, J. R. (2014) "Etheric Ocean," www.luckysoap.com/etherico cean/index.html.

Cayley, John (2007) "riverIsland," www.shadoof.net/in/riverisland.html.

Cramer, Kathryn (2012) "Am I Free to Go?," www.tor.com/2012/12/12/ am-i-free-to-go.

Cramer, Kathryn (2020) "Lizard Dreams," www.kathryncramer.com /kathryn_cramer/collage.

Falco, Edward (1997) *A Dream with Demons*. Watertown, MA: Eastgate Systems.

Jackson, Shelley (1995) *Patchwork Girl, Or A Modern Monster*. Watertown, MA: Eastgate Systems.

Joyce, Michael (1987) *afternoon, a story*. Watertown, MA: Eastgate Systems.

Larsen, Deena (2000) *Disappearing Rain*. www.deenalarsen.net/rain

Larsen, Deena (2012) *Marble Springs 3.0*. http://marblesprings.wikidot.com

Malin, Heather (1999) "contour and consciousness," unpublished Storyspace hypertext.

McDaid, John (1992) *Uncle Buddy's Phantom Funhouse*. Watertown, MA: Eastgate Systems.

Mencía, María (2001) "Birds Singing Other Birds' Songs," in N. Katherine Hayles, Nick Montfort, Scott Rettberg, and Stephanie Strickland (eds.), *Electronic Literature Collection Vol. 1*. https://collection .eliterature.org/1/works/mencia__birds_singing_other_birds_ songs.html

Moran, Monika (1993) *Ambulance: An Electronic Novel*. New York: Electronic Hollywood.

Moulthrop, Stuart (1991) *Victory Garden*. Watertown, MA: Eastgate Systems.

Strickland, Stephanie (1997) *True North*. Watertown, MA: Eastgate Systems.

Secondary Works

Aarseth, Espen (1997) *Cybertext: Perspectives on Ergodic Literature*. Baltimore, MD: Johns Hopkins University Press.

Barthes, Roland (1970) *S/Z*. New York: Hill & Wang.

Barthes, Roland (1977) *Image – Music – Text*, ed. and trans. Stephen Heath. New York: Hill & Wang.

Bell, Alice, Astrid Ensslin, Dave Ciccoricco, Jess Laccetti, Jessica Pressman, and Hans Rustad (2010) "A [S]creed for Digital Fiction," *electronic book review*, March 7. www.electronicbookreview.com/thread/electropoe tics/DFINative

Bernstein, Mark (2016) "Storyspace 3," *HT '16: Proceedings of the 27th ACM Conference on Hypertext and Social Media*, July 2016, pp. 201–2016. https://doi.org/10.1145/2914586.2914624

Bolter, Jay David, and Richard Grusin (1997) *Remediation: Understanding New Media*. Cambridge, MA: MIT Press.

Bootz, P. (2005) "Transitoire Observable: A Laboratory for Emergent Programmed Art," *dichtung digital*. www.dichtung-digital.de/2005/1/Bootz/index.htm

CDS, Brown University (1999) "futureTEXT: Jim Rosenberg on Hypertext Fiction," Technology Platforms for 21st Century Literature Conference, April 7. https://vimeo.com/12771049

Chartier, Roger (1994) *The Order of Books: Readers, Authors, and Libraries in Europe between the Fourteenth and Eighteenth Centuries*. Stanford, CA: Stanford University Press.

Conklin, Jeff (1987) "Hypertext: A Survey and Introduction," *IEEE Computer*, 20 (9): 17–41.

Coover, Robert (1992) "The End of Books," *New York Times*, June 21. https://archive.nytimes.com/www.nytimes.com/books/98/09/27/specials/coover-end.html

Coover, Robert (1993) "Hyperfiction: Novels for the Computer," New York Times on the Web, August 29. https://archive.nytimes.com/www.nytimes.com/books/98/09/27/specials/coover-hyperfiction.html

Davenport, Guy (1981) "Narrative Tone and Form," in *The Geography of the Imagination*. San Francisco: North Point Press, pp. 308–318.

Deleuze, Gille, and Félix Guattari (1987) *A Thousand Plateaus: Capitalism and Schizophrenia*, trans. and foreword B. Massumi. Minneapolis: University of Minneapolis Press.

di Rosario, Giovanna (2017) "Gender As Patterns: Unfixed Forms in Electronic Poetry," in María Mencía (ed.), *#WomenTechLit*, Morgantown: West Virginia University Press, pp. 41–54.

Drouin, Jeffrey, and Matthew J. Huculak (2016) "Little Magazines," in Stephen Ross (ed.), *Routledge Encyclopedia of Modernism*. doi:10.4324/9781135000356-REM979-1

Duguid, Paul (2006) "Material Matters: The Past and Futurology of the Book," in D. Finkelstein and A. McCleery (eds.), *The Book History Reader*, 2nd ed., Abingdon: Routledge.

Ensslin, Astrid (2007) *Canonizing Hypertext: Explorations and Constructions*. London: Bloomsbury.

(2014) *Literary Gaming*. Cambridge, MA: MIT Press.

(2019) "Intergrams," Electronic Literature Directory, https://directory.eliterature.org/individual-work/5038.

(2020a), "'Completing the Circle'? The Curious Counter-canonical Case of the *Eastgate Quarterly Review of Hypertext* (1994–1995)", in Bertrand Gervais and Sophie Marcotte (eds.), *Attention à la marche! Mind the Gap! Thinking Electronic Literature in a Digital Culture*, Les Presses the l'Écureuil, pp. 511–524.

(2020b) "Hypertext Theory," in John Frow, Mark Byron, Pelagia Goulimari, Sean Pryor, and Julie Rak (eds.), *The Oxford Encyclopedia of Literature*. https://oxfordre.com/literature/view/10.1093/acrefore/9780190201098.001.0001/acrefore-9780190201098-e-982

Ensslin, Astrid, and Alice Bell (2021) *Digital Fiction and the Unnatural: Transmedial Narrative Theory, Method and Analysis*. Columbus: Ohio State University Press.

Ensslin, Astrid, and Lyle Skains (2017) "Hypertext: Storyspace to Twine," in J. Tabbi (ed.), *The Bloomsbury Handbook of Electronic Literature*. New York: Bloomsbury, pp. 295–310.

Feldman, Shoshana (1985) *Writing and Madness: Literature/Philosophy/Psychoanalysis*. Stanford, CA: Stanford University Press.

Forster, E. M. (1927) *Aspects of the Novel*. London: Edward Arnold.

Funkhouser, Chris (2007) *Prehistoric Digital Poetry*. Tuscaloosa: University of Alabama Press.

Genette, Gérard. 1979. *Introduction à l'architexte*. Paris: Éditions du Seuil.

Gess, Richard (1993) "Mahasukha Halo." *Leonardo*, 26(3), 257–258.

Glazier, Loss P. (2001) *Digital Poetics: The Making of E-Poetries*. Tuscaloosa: University of Alabama Press.

Grigar, Dene (2018a) "Love and Loss in Kendall's A Life Set for Two," Electronic Literature Lab, April 5, 2018, https://dtc-wsuv.org/wp/ell/2018/04/05/metaphor-in-kendalls-a-life-set-for-two

(2018b) "Repetition in Mary-Kim Arnold's "Lust," in Grigar et al. (eds.), *Rebooting Electronic Literature 1: Documenting Born Digital Pre-Web Media*, https://elmcip.net/critical-writing/rebooting-electronic-literature-documenting-pre-web-born-digital-media-volume-1

(2018c) "Critical Essay about J. Yellowlees Douglas' I Have Said Nothing," in Grigar et al. (eds.), *Rebooting Electronic Literature 1: Documenting Born Digital Pre-Web Media*, https://scalar.usc.edu/works/rebooting-electronic-literature/critical-essays-about-jane-yellowlees-douglas-i-have-said-nothing?path=jane-yellowlees-douglas-i-have-said-nothing

(2018d) "Traversal of Robert Kendall's A Life Set for Two, Introduction." https://vimeo.com/265834376

(2019) "A Conversation about Socrates in the Labyrinth, Hypertext, & the Lore of Electronic Literature." https://vimeo.com/358533888

Grigar, Dene, Kathy Mac, Astrid Ensslin, Mariusz Pisarski, and John Barber (2021a) "Traversal of Kathy Mac's 'Unnatural Habitats'," video, Electronic Literature Lab, Washington State

University Vancouver, July 2nd. www.youtube.com/watch?v=cq8o2eM7Lkg

Grigar, Dene, and Stuart Moulthrop (2017) *Pathfinders*. http://dtc-wsuv.org/wp/pathfinders/

Grigar, Dene, and Nicholas Schiller (2018) "Traversal of Mary Kim Arnold's 'Lust,'" *Electronic Literature Lab*, *WSUV*, May 18. www.youtube.com/watch?v=gVgVj4JjbUQ

Grigar, Dene, Nicholas Schiller, Vanessa Rhodes, Veronica Whitney, Mariah Gwin, and Katie Bowen (2018) *Rebooting Electronic Literature: Documenting Pre-Web Born Digital Media, Volume 1*. https://scalar.usc.edu/works/rebooting-electronic-literature/index

Grigar, Dene, Nicholas Schiller, Holly Slocum, Mariah Gwin, Andrew Nevue, Kathleen Zoller, and Moneca Roath (2019) *Rebooting Electronic Literature: Documenting Pre-web Born Digital Media, Volume 2*. https://scalar.usc.edu/works/rebooting-electronic-literature-volume-2/index

Grigar, Dene, Holly Slocum, Kathleen Zoller, Nicholas Schiller, Moneca Roath, and Mariah Gwin (2020) *Rebooting Electronic Literature: Dcoumenting Pre-web Born Digital Media, Volume 3*. https://scalar.usc.edu/works/rebooting-electronic-literature-volume-3/index

Grigar, Dene, Richard Smyth, Astrid Ensslin, Mariusz Pisarski, and John Barber (2021b) "Traversal of Richard Smyth's 'Genetis: A Rhizography,'" video, Electronic Literature Lab, Washington State University Vancouver, June 25. www.youtube.com/watch?v=IiS0wmRDxTg

Hayles, N. Katherine (1993) "Virtual Bodies and Flickering Signifiers." *October*, 66, 69–91.

(2002) *Writing Machines*. Cambridge, MA: MIT Press.

(2004) "Print Is Flat, Code Is Deep: The Importance of Media-Specific Analysis." *Poetics Today*, 25:1.

(2008) *Electronic Literature: New Horizons for the Literary*. South Bend, IN: Notre Dame University Press.

Higgason, Richard E. (2004) "The Mystery of 'Lust,'" HYPERTEXT '04: Proceedings of the Fifteenth ACM Conference on Hypertext and Hypermedia, August, pp. 28–35. https://doi.org/10.1145/1012807.1012818

Joyce, Michael (2000) *Othermindedness: The Emergence of Network Culture*. Ann Arbor: University of Michigan Press.

Kittler, Friedrich (1992) *Discourse Networks, 1800/1900*. Stanford, CA: Stanford University Press.

Lacan, Jacques (1994) *Le Séminaire: Livre IV. La relation d'objet, 1956–1957*, ed. Jacques-Alain Miller. Paris; Seuil.

Landow, George P. (1997) *Hypertext 2.0: The Convergence of Contemporary Critical Theory and Technology*. Baltimore, MD: Johns Hopkins University Press.

(2006) *Hypertext 3.0: Critical Theory and New Media in an Era of Globalization*. Baltimore, MD: Johns Hopkins University Press.

madeApple.com (2020) "Macintosh Performa 5215CD", https://madeapple.com/macintosh-performa-5215cd/

McGann, Jerome J. (1991) *The Textual Condition*. Princeton, NJ: Princeton University Press.

Moulthrop, Stuart, and Dene Grigar (2017) *Traversals: The Use of Preservation for Early Electronic Writing*. Cambridge, MA: MIT Press.

Murray, Mary (1994) *The Law of the Father? Patriarchy in the Transition from Feudalism to Capitalism*. New York: Routledge.

Pressman, Jessica (2014) *Digital Modernism: Making It New in New Media*. Oxford: Oxford University Press.

(2020) *Bookishness: Loving Books in a Digital Age*. New York: Columbia University Press.

Rettberg, Scott (2019) *Electronic Literature*. Cambridge: Polity.

Richards, I. A. (1924) *Principles of Literary Criticism*. Abingdon: Routledge & Kegan Paul.

Rosenberg, Jim (1994) "Navigating Nowhere / Hypertext Infrawhere." *ACM SIGlink Newsletter*, 3:3, www.inframergence.org/jr/NNHI .html

(1996) "The Interactive Diagram Sentence: Hypertext As a Medium of Thought." *Visible Language*, 30:2, 102–117. www.inframergence.org/ jr/VL.html

(2015) *Jim Rosenberg*, personal website, www.inframergence.org.

Ryan, Marie-Laure (2006) *Avatars of Story*. Minneapolis: University of Minnesota Press.

Ryan, Marie-Laure, and Jan-Noël Thon (2014) *Storyworlds across Media: Toward a Media-Conscious Narratology*. Lincoln: University of Nebraska Press.

Salter, Anastasia (2015) "Alice in Dataland," *Kairos*, 20:1. http://kairos .technorhetoric.net/20.1/inventio/salter/index.html

Schweikle, Günther and Irmgard Schweikle (1990) *Metzler Literatur Lexikon*. Stuttgart: Metzler.

Slocum, Holly (2019) "Samplers: Nine Vicious Little Hypertexts," Electronic Literature Directory, November 9. https://directory .eliterature.org/individual-work/5051

Smyth, Richard (1994) "Renaissance Mnemonics, Poststructuralism, and the Rhetoric of Hypertext Composition," PhD dissertation, University of Florida. https://dl.acm.org/doi/book/10.5555/922731

Sullivan, Laura L. (1999) "Wired Women Writing: Towards a Feminist Theorization of Hypertext," *Computers and Composition*, 16:1, 25–54. https://doi.org/10.1016/S8755-4615(99)80004-8

Swigart, Rob (2020) "Other Media," *Rob Swigart: Words That Matter*. www .robswigart.com/games-and-interactive-media

Tabbi, Joseph (2010) "Electronic Literature As World Literature; or, The Universality of Writing under Constraint," *Poetics Today*, 31:1.

Thomas, Bronwen, Julia Round, and Astrid Ensslin (eds.) (forthcoming) *The Routledge Handbook of Literary Media*. New York: Routledge.

Tomaszek, Patricia (2014) "In the Absence of the Publisher's Peritext," paper given at "Paratext in Digital Culture" workshop, University of Bergen, August 2014.

Ulmer, Gregory (2003) *Internet Invention: From Literacy to Electracy*. New York: Longman.

Waterman, Sue (2009) "Literary Journals," in Lisa Block de Behar, Paola Mildonian, Jean-Michel Dijan, Djelal Kadir, Alfons Knauth, Dolores Romero Lopez, and Márcio Seligmann Silva (eds.), *Comparative Literature: Sharing Knowledges for Preserving Cultural Diversity*. Rio de Janeiro: Encyclopedia of Life Support Systems. www .eolss.net/Sample-Chapters/C04/E6-87-04-03.pdf

Wollaeger, Mark, and Kevin J. H. Dettmar (2014) "Series Editors' Foreword," in J. Pressman, *Digital Modernism*, pp. ix–xii.

Zimmer, Carl, "Floppy Fiction," *Discover* Vol. 10, Issue 11, November 1989, pp. 34–36.

Zipes, Jack (2006) *Fairy Tales and the Art of Subversion: The Classical Genre for Children and the Process of Civilization*. 2nd ed. New York: Taylor & Francis.

Acknowledgments

This Element owes its genesis to several wonderful people, to whom I am infinitely indebted. First, I want to thank Dene Grigar and John Barber for hosting my visiting fellowship at WSU Vancouver in August 2019, and to Dene in particular for giving me access to the precious resources of the Electronic Literature Lab. My thanks goes to the entire ELL team for providing inspiration and support, and especially to Moneca Roath for recording my traversals, and to Greg Philbrook, Nicholas Schiller, and Holly Slocum for food for thought, technical support, and entertainment.

This work is a collaborative effort in the lore of electronic literature, and I want to extend my gratitude to all interviewees and interlocutors who informed and critiqued this study: Mary-Kim Arnold, Mark Bernstein, Kathryn Cramer, J. Yellowlees Douglas, Edward Falco, Richard Gess, Diane Greco, Michael Joyce, Robert Kendall, Deena Larsen, Heather Malin, Kathleen McConnell, Stuart Moulthrop, Jim Rosenberg, Richard Smyth, Rob Swigart, and Michael van Mantgem. Further thanks goes to Emily Villanueva for her assistance with data transcription, and to Alice Bell and Deena Larsen for editorial advice. The Cambridge University Press Elements "Publishing and Book Culture" team, led by Samantha Rayner and Leah Tether, lent their patience, support, and feedback, and the Press's editors and proofreaders improved the manuscript through meticulous copy-editing support. Finally, I want to thank Atik, Anton, and Leo, who supported me at a time when pandemic restrictions and a cross-continental move threw spanner after spanner into the works, and to the Digital Culture group at the University of Bergen, led by Scott Rettberg and Jill Walker-Rettberg, for providing a new home for my research.

Cambridge Elements ☰

Publishing and Book Culture

SERIES EDITOR

Samantha Rayner
University College London

Samantha Rayner is Professor of Publishing and Book Cultures at UCL. She is also Director of UCL's Centre for Publishing, co-Director of the Bloomsbury CHAPTER (Communication History, Authorship, Publishing, Textual Editing and Reading) and co-Chair of the Bookselling Research Network.

ASSOCIATE EDITOR

Leah Tether
University of Bristol

Leah Tether is Professor of Medieval Literature and Publishing at the University of Bristol. With an academic background in medieval French and English literature and a professional background in trade publishing, Leah has combined her expertise and developed an international research profile in book and publishing history from manuscript to digital.

ADVISORY BOARD

Simone Murray, Monash University

Claire Squires, University of Stirling

Andrew Nash, University of London

Leslie Howsam, Ryerson University

David Finkelstein, University of Edinburgh

Alexis Weedon, University of Bedfordshire

Alan Staton, Booksellers Association

Angus Phillips, Oxford International Centre for Publishing

Richard Fisher, Yale University Press

John Maxwell, Simon Fraser University

Shafquat Towheed, The Open University

Jen McCall, Emerald Publishing

About the series

This series aims to fill the demand for easily accessible, quality texts available for teaching and research in the diverse and dynamic fields of Publishing and Book Culture. Rigorously researched and peer-reviewed Elements will be published under themes, or 'Gatherings'. These Elements should be the first check point for researchers or students working on that area of publishing and book trade history and practice: we hope that, situated so logically at Cambridge University Press, where academic publishing in the UK began, it will develop to create an unrivalled space where these histories and practices can be investigated and preserved.

Cambridge Elements ☰

Publishing and Book Culture

Digital Literary Culture

Gathering Editor: Laura Dietz

Laura Dietz is a Senior Lecturer in Writing and Publishing in the Cambridge School of Creative Industries at Anglia Ruskin University. She writes novels and studies novels, publishing fiction alongside research on topics such as e-novel readership, the digital short story, online literary magazines, and the changing definition of authorship in the digital era.

ELEMENTS IN THE GATHERING

The Network Turn: Changing Perspectives in the Humanities
Ruth Ahnert, Sebastian E. Ahnert, Catherine Nicole Coleman and Scott B. Weingart

Reading Computer-Generated Texts
Leah Henrickson

Pre-web Digital Publishing and the Lore of Electronic Literature
Astrid Ensslin

A full series listing is available at: www.cambridge.org/EPBC

Printed in the United States
by Baker & Taylor Publisher Services